THINGS HIDDEN COMPANION GUIDE

By Richard Rohr

The Tears of Things: Prophetic Wisdom for an Age of Outrage

*The Universal Christ: How a Forgotten Reality Can Change
Everything We See, Hope For, and Believe*

*Every Thing Is Sacred: 40 Practices and Reflections
on the Universal Christ*

Breathing Under Water: Spirituality and the Twelve Steps

Breathing Under Water Companion Journal

Eager to Love: The Alternative Way of Francis of Assisi

*Eager to Love Companion Guide:
Prompts and Reflection for Contemplation*

From Wild Man to Wise Man: Reflections on Male Spirituality

The Great Themes of Scripture: Old Testament

The Great Themes of Scripture: New Testament

Jesus' Alternative Plan: The Sermon on the Mount

Preparing for Christmas: Daily Meditations for Advent

Silent Compassion: Finding God in Contemplation

Things Hidden: Scripture as Spirituality

Things Hidden Companion Guide

Why Be Catholic?: Understanding Our Experience and Tradition

The Wisdom Pattern: Order, Disorder, Reorder

Wondrous Encounters: Scripture for Lent

Yes, And . . . : Daily Meditations

THINGS HIDDEN
COMPANION GUIDE

SCRIPTURE AS SPIRITUALITY

RICHARD ROHR

CONVERGENT
NEW YORK

Convergent
An imprint of Random House
A division of Penguin Random House LLC
1745 Broadway, New York, NY 10019
convergentbooks.com
penguinrandomhouse.com

Unless otherwise stated, Richard Rohr uses his own translation and/or paraphrase of Scripture. Father Richard draws from a variety of English translations, including the Jerusalem Bible (JB), New American Standard Bible (NASB), New English Translation (NET), J.B. Phillips New Testament (Phillips), Revised Standard Version (RSV), and The Message (MSG).

2026 Convergent Books Trade Paperback Edition

Originally published in paperback in the United States by Franciscan Media, in 2023.

ISBN 979-8-217-42375-0
Ebook ISBN 979-8-217-42376-7

Printed in the United States of America

1st Printing

Book Team: Production editor: Michelle Daniel • Managing editor: Allison Fox • Production manager: Linnea Knollmueller

Book design by Mark Sullivan

The authorized representative in the EU for product safety and compliance is Penguin Random House Ireland, Morrison Chambers, 32 Nassau Street, Dublin D02 YH68, Ireland. https://eu-contact.penguin.ie

As Richard Rohr writes in *Things Hidden: Scripture as Spirituality*, his desire "is to make some clear connections between what I perceive to be the prime ideas in the Judeo-Christian Scriptures and a practical and pastoral spirituality for believers today" (p. xiv). This Things Hidden Companion Guide, based in the pedagogy of the Center for Action and Contemplation (CAC), is a supportive tool for taking these connections more profoundly into your hearts and responding with transformed lives.

We are grateful for the opportunity to utilize the work of Patrick Boland, a longtime student and friend of Fr. Richard and an Executive Coach and Psychotherapist at Conexus in Dublin, Ireland, and Kirsten Oates, former Managing Director of Program Design at the CAC. Their pedagogical framework provides the structure for this Companion Guide.

Shirin McArthur, former CAC staff member, spiritual director, retreat leader, and editor at Shirin McArthur Ministries, chose the excerpted quotations from *Things Hidden* and crafted the reflection questions, invitations, and activities.

I also am thankful for my longtime collaborative relationship with Vanessa Guerin, Director of Publications for the CAC, who shepherded the creative process for this Companion Guide and edited the initial draft.

We are so grateful for the deep study and prayerful inspiration that Fr. Richard put into *Things Hidden*. Through this Companion Guide, we hope that you will more fully experience the transformative connections between spirituality and the Scriptures.

—Diane M. Houdek

Content Director

Franciscan Media

CONTENTS

Welcome to this Companion Guide for *Things Hidden: Scripture as Spirituality*. We strongly encourage you to read this introduction as an investment in your full participation in each chapter of *Things Hidden*.

The goal of this guide is to deepen your understanding and experience of the major themes identified by Fr. Richard Rohr as woven through the Bible and apply them in your daily life. It is both a *meditation* on many of the important concepts in the book and an *invitation* to holistically experience a deepening connection with God.

Through engagement with this Companion Guide, you can:

- further reflect on the major themes running through the Hebrew and Christian Scriptures;
- learn and engage in Christian contemplative practices that deepen these reflections;
- set intentions for becoming a more loving, engaged presence in the world.

Although some of the questions are typical of study guides you might have used in the past, many of the questions seek to move us beyond focusing on our thoughts and reflections to a more holistic, embodied experience of the reality toward which Fr. Richard is pointing in *Things Hidden*.

In addition to these instructions for using this companion guide as an individual, there are instructions at the back of this book for using this guide with groups.

Suggested Supplies to Fully Engage with This Companion Guide

- journal and pen
- timer
- Bible
- *Things Hidden* book
- Companion Guide
- candle

Journal and Pen

You will need a journal to record your thoughts and responses to the various questions in the guide. This can help you notice how both your experience and understanding are deepening as you move through the book.

Timer

You will need a digital prayer bell or other (gentle) timer to signal the start and end of the contemplative sit exercises. This will help you to fully engage in the self-guided contemplative sits without having to check the time remaining for each exercise.

Bible

It will be important to have a Bible or Bible app available for Scripture readings and reflection.

Things Hidden Book and Companion Guide

Each chapter of this Companion Guide corresponds with a chapter in *Things Hidden*. It is important to read each chapter of *Things Hidden* prior to engaging with that chapter in the Companion Guide.

Candle

Depending on your preference and tradition, the simple act of lighting a candle might symbolize your entry into a focused time of conscious reflection.

Regular Routine and Timing

Developing a regular routine could be of help as you work through this Companion Guide. You may wish to consider:

- Choosing a particular place where you will engage with the Companion Guide. This would ideally be somewhere quiet, where you will not be disturbed (for example, an oratory or chapel, a quiet coffee shop, a place in nature, or a room in your home where you feel most at ease).
- Finding a time slot that you can schedule on a recurring basis.
- Determining how to begin each period of reflection (for example, turning off your phone, taking a moment of silence to "arrive," lighting a candle, journaling about how you are feeling, etc.).
- Deciding how to end each time of reflection (for example, extinguishing the candle, journaling beyond the Companion Guide questions, praying in a way that is most familiar to you, etc.).
- Transitioning back to the rest of your day with a particular activity (for example, praying for others who are using this Companion Guide, engaging in an act of service, going for a walk, having breakfast/coffee/dinner to ease you back into your day, etc.).

Although your lifestyle may not always allow it, developing a regular routine will likely help you to commit to engaging with this Companion Guide in the most personally meaningful way possible.

The amount of time you need to spend on each chapter of the Companion Guide will vary. A good rule of thumb is not to move on to the next question until you feel you have, at least to some extent, digested what you sense the question is about. Sometimes you may wish to go back and reread sections of *Things Hidden* before responding to a reflection question or engaging in an exercise. This will take additional time. We suggest that you take this process at your own pace, which will be more satisfying and impactful than "rushing" questions in an attempt to "complete" the Companion Guide within a certain period of time.

What to Expect from this Companion Guide

This is an experiential Companion Guide. We encourage you to engage in each of the contemplative sits and *lectio* practices (these will be fully described below). This is in keeping with the tone and message of Fr. Richard's commitment to both action and contemplation, study and practice. Our faith deepens as much from our approach to spirituality (experiential knowledge) as from our approach to theology (cognitive knowledge). Contemplative sits and *lectio* practices train our mind to be more aware of our experience and open our hearts to God's presence. Detailed instructions are provided throughout the Companion Guide.

There are quite a few questions for each chapter and they will take some time to complete. Rather than setting a strict time period for working with each chapter, we encourage you to go at your own pace, being present to the material and not rushing through any of the content.

As you read through each question in this Companion Guide, take your time to read slowly and do not move on until some part of you has resonated with the quotations and the accompanying questions or instructions.

You do not need to thoroughly complete this Companion Guide in order to assimilate Fr. Richard's book. However, if you find yourself skipping questions, it might be interesting to notice if there is a pattern emerging in the theme or style of these questions and/or your response to them.

There is enough content here to last several weeks or even months of dedicated reflection. Give yourself permission to take your time and proceed in a manner that is meaningful for you. Scripture study is a lifelong process. It could take many years for you to absorb and incorporate each of Fr. Richard's themes into your everyday life. You may wish to return to this book and Companion Guide on a yearly basis.

The quotations and p. numbers from *Things Hidden* reflect the revised version (2022 edition) of the book.

Overview to Engaging in the Practices

Reflection

Most exercises in this Companion Guide take the form of a reflection. You will be presented with a quotation from *Things Hidden* and two or more questions for reflection from that piece of text.

These reflection questions are designed to help you process the content of the book at a deeper level than if you were to simply read the book on its own.

The intention of each reflection exercise is twofold: to help you think through the concepts contained within *Things Hidden* and to notice what you feel and experience as a result.

Journaling

You might find it helpful to journal regularly as you journey through the book and Companion Guide. This optional spiritual practice can facilitate your meditation on the concepts in the book and deepen your connection with God.

Your journal entry might be single words or long sentences, artwork or doodling, or whatever feels appropriate. Please note that these are only suggestions; of greater importance is that you do not feel any pressure to "complete" journal entries, but feel free to process the reflections in whichever way(s) you find helpful.

Activity

Some exercises in this Companion Guide center around or include an activity that expands the field of participation beyond reading, writing, contemplation, and response. The intent is to deepen your full-body engagement with the content of the book by utilizing other senses and stimuli. As with everything in this Companion Guide, feel free to adjust these activities to accommodate your abilities and comfort level (see more on this below).

Lectio Practice

Lectio divina is a practice of reading, meditating on, and praying with Scripture. The Latin term *lectio divina* literally means a Divine Lesson. The practice originated where faith communities engaged in the sacred reading of biblical texts in the hope of receiving a divine lesson from God.

Lectio divina can also be translated as "spiritual reading" or "sacred reading," which refer to the practice of reading other spiritual texts. Most of the *lectio divina* texts in this Companion Guide come from *Things Hidden*. As such, these exercises are termed *lectio* practices, an umbrella term that includes both sacred Scripture and Fr. Richard's book.

There are four rounds of textual reading in each of the *lectio* practices in this guide. The four rounds follow a simple format:

1. With the first reading, allow yourself to *settle in* to the exercise and familiarize yourself with the words. Read the text out loud, slowly and clearly. Pause for a breath or two before moving on.

It's important to read at an appropriate pace that sets the tone for your intention. Reading each round out loud will help you to identify the word or phrase that most speaks to you from the text. Silent pauses are particularly important between each of the four rounds.

2. For the second reading, *listen* from a centered heart space and notice any word or phrase that stands out to you.

Between the first and second round of reading, you are encouraged to pause for long enough to really feel like you have settled into the text. This will enable a particular quality of listening, from a centered heart space, that will help you to connect with a certain word or phrase.

3. After a few moments of silence, read the text a third time, *reflecting* on how this word or phrase is connected to your current life experience. Take a minute to linger over this word or phrase and allow it to engage your body, heart, and awareness of the world around you.

You may want to speak a response aloud or write something in your journal.

This is the round where you seek to uncover some of the reasons for the resonance you are experiencing with this word or phrase. Sometimes the connection is clear. At other times, it may not be clear why a particular word or phrase stood out for you.

The invitation is for you to reflect for a few moments, but not to overthink it. Sometimes the word or phrase will return to you in the days and weeks ahead—and only then will you realize why it was meaningful for you. As Fr. Richard notes, "we are always ready to be surprised and graced by the Unfamiliar, which is why it is called 'faith' to begin with" (p. xiii).

4. For the final reading, *respond* with a prayer or expression of what you have experienced, inviting the infinite wisdom of God to support you in places of unknowing, confusion, desire, or hope.

Building on the previous rounds, this final reading focuses on expressing your response to the exercise. Sometimes you may feel hopeful or desirous of something and will want to make a request of God in prayer. At other times you might feel confused and unsure about the entire exercise. These can often be fruitful times of prayer and response. You might choose a written journal entry, a vocal prayer, or even a contemplative sit. Please select a response that best suits you and encourages your connection with the hidden things in Scripture and your life.

Contemplative Sit

A contemplative sit is a spiritual discipline and form of prayer with the aim being to draw you "into more interior, meditative ways of experiencing God's presence"[1] in your life. It involves your remaining silent and open, in God's presence, to having your brain rewired "to think non-dually with compassion, kindness, and a lack of attachment to the ego's preferences."[2]

---

1. James Finley, *Christian Meditation: Experiencing the Presence of God* (New York: HarperCollins, 2004), 24.
2. "Contemplation," *Center for Action and Contemplation*, https://cac.org/about-cac/contemplation/.

As Fr. Richard teaches in *Things Hidden*:

The ancient teaching on contemplation, as well as its practice, was largely lost for centuries until Thomas Merton began to retrieve it in the twentieth century. He pointed out that even formal "contemplative" orders were largely working inside the *kataphatic* [imaged, verbal] tradition, and had little training in the older practice of non-dual consciousness and non-wordy knowing. Many saints and mystics did become contemplatives, but largely by grace ["infused contemplation"] rather than any formal or refined teaching. Contemplation has since been revived by such teachers as John Main, Thomas Keating, Cynthia Bourgeault, Ruth Burrows, and Laurence Freeman, sometimes under the rubric of "Centering Prayer." (p. 131)

"Fr. Richard often says that contemplation is an exercise in failure."[3] This is because, each time we pray and despite "our best intentions to remain present to Presence, our habitual patterns of thinking and feeling interrupt and distract. Yet it is the desire that matters, and through our failing we encounter God's grace."[4]

The contemplative sit exercises in this Companion Guide are designed to develop or deepen your practice of this form of prayerful openness to God and, as such, are very intentionally structured. Contemplative sits appear in each chapter of the Companion Guide, along with instructions that can be read either silently or aloud.

Timing

The first sit, in chapter one, suggests beginners start with a period of five minutes. For those who are more familiar with

---

3. "Contemplation."
4. "Contemplation."

this meditative practice, we recommend engaging in a contemplative sit for a period of twenty or even thirty minutes. As the Companion Guide progresses, the recommended minimum time for each sit increases, moving to ten minutes, then fifteen, and finally to twenty. Please feel free to increase the amount of time for your sit to twenty minutes as soon as you feel ready.

Instructions for Each Sit

The instructions for contemplative sit are outlined every time it occurs in the Companion Guide. The Appendix includes a fuller set of instructions to guide those who are unfamiliar with the practice or wish some reminders on important points.

Staying within Your Comfort Zone

If any aspect of the self-guided instructions throughout this Companion Guide are unhelpful or off-putting for you, please feel completely free to change the approach to suit your needs. There are many people that have unhealed pain or trauma in their lives that might be triggered by certain body postures, breathing techniques, or imagination exercises, so it will be important for you to adapt those instructions to your particular circumstances.

Such pain or trauma could be from a childhood experience or more recent events. It might be something of which you are fully aware, or it might be hidden in your body. As you enter into a contemplative practice, the pain or trauma can unexpectedly arise and cause overwhelming sensations. For example, you might start an exercise and begin to experience very negative emotions or sensations (such as dizziness, rage, intense crying, hyperventilation, or disconnection from your body).

Of most importance is that you do not push yourself beyond your comfort zone. If you find that you are regularly experiencing overwhelming emotions or physical sensations, we recommend that you stop using the Companion Guide and discuss these experiences with a mental health professional (for example, a counsellor, psychotherapist, or psychiatrist). However, if you have the capacity to work with what is arising, below are some adaptations and interventions you could try.

During the practice:

- Keep your eyes open.
- Shift your attention from your breath and choose to focus on what you can hear or see.
- Change the position of your body during the practice (for example, stand up, lie down, walk around).
- Find a different room or place to practice.
- Choose a new sacred word.
- Instead of choosing a word, use one or more of your five senses to refocus your attention.
- Hold something, or place it beside you, that makes you feel safe and "at home" when you touch it.
- Shorten the time of your practice.

If you feel unexpectedly triggered, please consider supporting yourself in the following ways:

- Simply stop the contemplative sit or other spiritual practice.
- Speak aloud to yourself (for example, "It's ok, I'm ok. I am here now and safe in this moment, not trapped in a past experience that wasn't so safe.").
- Stand up and walk around.
- Touch the floor, the ground, or something with you that makes you feel safe and "at home" when you touch it.
- Smell something that brings good memories to mind (for example, a favorite food, fragrance, or essential oil).

- Listen to a piece of music or any sound that brings you a sense of calm.
- Look at a photo of someone or something that has very good memories or connotations for you.
- In the absence of a photo, picture in your mind's eye an image with good memories or connotations or say it aloud (for example, "The warm sun, the blue sea").

Again, as you work your way through this Companion Guide, do not push yourself beyond your comfort zone. Our hope is that you will feel very safe as you deepen your spiritual practice throughout this Companion Guide.

Connecting the Dots

1. Reflection

The first motion is already planted within us by God at our creation (see Jeremiah 1:5; Isaiah 49:1), and that is probably what gives spiritual wisdom both such inner conviction and such outer authority. I have always said that the best compliment I ever get is when people tell me something to this effect: "Richard, you did not teach me anything totally new. Somehow, I already knew it, but it did not become conscious or real for me until you said it." …

On some level, spiritual cognition is invariably experienced as "re-cognition." Even Peter said that his work was largely "recalling" and "reminding" (see 2 Peter 1:12–15) his people. For some reason, we have forgotten that. (p. xii)

Read these paragraphs again, then sit in silence for a few moments. When you are ready, reflect on the following questions, recording as much as you wish in your journal.

- When have you heard something that resonated for you in this way Fr. Richard describes? Recall as much as you can of that moment: the context, the teaching, and your felt response to that conscious recognition.
- What has helped or hindered your own experiences of "re-cognition"?

- Describe what it means to you that God plants wisdom within us in this way. How does this impact your openness and willingness to be guided by the Holy Spirit in reading Scripture?

2. Reflection

Slowly read over this quotation two or three times, then ponder the questions below.

> Our unwillingness, or our inability, to thin-slice the texts and then discern the tangents has created widespread fundamentalist Christianity, Judaism, and Islam, which, ironically, usually miss the "fundamentals"! *If we do not know the direction and the momentum, we will not recognize the backpedaling.* (p. xiii)

- What do you consider the "fundamentals" of your faith? How were they revealed to you? In what ways have these fundamentals changed and been challenged over the course of your life?
- When have you found yourself backpedaling in the spiritual life? How did you realize this was happening? What people or events helped you to move forward again, and how did that process unfold?

3. Reflection

> My desire here is to make some clear connections between what I perceive to be the prime ideas in the Judeo-Christian Scriptures and a practical and pastoral spirituality for believers today. (p. xiv)

Prayerfully reflect on your desire for engaging with Scripture through *Things Hidden* and this Companion Guide.

Write down your desire and re-read it each time you begin engaging with this Companion Guide. Notice whether and how any changes arise in that desire during the weeks you spend with this Companion Guide.

4. Reflection

Although my tangent definitely coalesces in Jesus, whom we Christians call the Christ, I would like to believe that a lover of the Hebrew Scriptures will also find much to relish here.

I love the clear continuities between the two Testaments and clearly see Jesus as first of all a Jew, who brilliantly thin-sliced his own tradition and gave us a wonderful lens by which to love the Jewish tradition and keep moving forward with it in an inclusive way (which became its child, Christianity). (pp. xiv–xv)

- Describe your relationship with the Hebrew Scriptures. How have they influenced and impacted your life—or not?
- What does it mean to focus on the fact that Jesus was a Jew? Spend some time in silence and notice which "clear continuities" rise from your Scripture reading or faith experience. What do they have to teach you in this moment?

5. Reflection

Only when inner and outer authority come together do we have true spiritual wisdom. We have for too long insisted on outer authority alone, without any teaching of prayer, inner journey, and maturing consciousness. The results for the world and for religion have been disastrous. (p. xv)

- In what ways have you trusted, or not trusted, both inner and outer authority? How and why has that changed over the course of your life?
- Describe what it would mean to you to accept Fr. Richard's invitation to trust your own inner authority.

6. Contemplative Sit

Leading in with the quotation below, practice a contemplative sit. You may wish to set a timer or digital prayer bell for five, ten, or twenty minutes, so that you know when to finish. If engaging in a contemplative sit is new to you, begin with five minutes.

- Seat yourself in a quiet area.
- Ground yourself and allow your breathing to settle.
- Notice any tightness in your shoulders and neck and allow any tension in your muscles to relax.
- Allow your back to rest in an aligned, neutral position.
- Once you are settled, read the following passage aloud— this is the opening text for your sit:

You will note that I use many Scripture citations with only a small comment, hoping that such a small comment will tease and invite you into deeper involvement with the text and context for yourself. I would love to inspire you to love Scripture, and go there for yourself, to find both your own inner experience named, and some outer validation of the same. (p. xv)

- Continue your sit in silence—focusing on your breath, connecting with your body, or by practicing any other method with which you are familiar.
- If a contemplative sit is new to you, one approach is to try not to let your attention attach to any thoughts, feelings, or sensations. Allow thoughts, feelings, and sensations to arise, exist, and then fall away while you keep your attention open and large, connecting to that much deeper consciousness.
- Remember, there is no goal. There is no right or wrong way—simply *be* present to what *is* in the moment.

Once finished, you may wish to journal your reflections on this experience.

CHAPTER ONE

INFORMATION IS NOT NECESSARILY TRANSFORMATION

1. Contemplative Sit

Leading in with the quotation below, practice a contemplative sit. You may wish to set a timer or digital prayer bell for five, ten, or twenty minutes, so that you know when to finish. If engaging in a contemplative sit is new to you, begin with five minutes.

- Seat yourself in a quiet area.
- Ground yourself and allow your breathing to settle.
- Notice any tightness in your shoulders and neck and allow any tension in your muscles to relax.
- Allow your back to rest in an aligned, neutral position.
- Once you are settled, read the following passage aloud— this is the opening text for your sit:

We need transformed people today, not just people with answers. (p. 1)

- Continue your sit in silence—focusing on your breath, connecting with your body, or by practicing any other method with which you are familiar.
- If a contemplative sit is new to you, one approach is to try not to let your attention attach to any thoughts, feelings, or sensations. Allow thoughts, feelings, and sensations to arise, exist, and then fall away while you keep your

attention open and large, connecting to that much deeper consciousness.

- Remember, there is no goal. There is no right or wrong way—simply *be* present to what *is* in the moment.

Once finished, you may wish to journal your reflections on this experience.

2. Reflection

Read the following paragraphs, then reflect on the questions below, recording as much as you wish in your journal.

> This marvelous anthology of books and letters called the Bible is all for the sake of astonishment. It's for divine transformation (*theosis*), not intellectual or "small-self" coziness....
>
> The biblical revelation invites us into a genuinely new experience. Wonderfully enough, human consciousness in the twenty-first century is, more than ever, ready for such an experience—and also very much in need of it! The trouble is that we have made the Bible into a bunch of ideas—about which we can be right or wrong—rather than an invitation to a *new set of eyes*. (pp. 1–2)

- How would you describe the Bible to someone who has never encountered it? Notice the differences between your description and Fr. Richard's.
- When has the Bible led you "into a genuinely new experience"? Describe as much of that experience as you can recall, then sit for a few moments in silence to see what else arises of that memory. What does it have to say to you today?
- When have you witnessed the Bible being reduced to "intellectual or 'small-self' coziness"? Were you aware of it at

the time, or only in retrospect? In what ways can you be careful to avoid such reduction in your own faith journey?

3. Reflection and Activity

We all always need what Jesus described as the beginner's mind of a curious child. A beginner's mind of what some call *constantly renewed immediacy* is the best path for spiritual wisdom. (p. 2)

- What components of the child's mind do you think Jesus is referring to? While we don't want to lose all our adult faculties, what have you lost from childhood that you might want to regain?
- Imagine what it would mean to you, on both the literal and figurative levels, to have the mind of a child.
- Write down a description of how such a "beginner's mind" could function.
- Find a child's game and play it. Can you let go of the need to "win" and focus on being present and open to whatever the game brings to you?

4. Reflection

We must know that for most of human history God was not a likeable, much less a lovable, character. That's why every biblical "theophany" (an event where God breaks through into history) begins with the same words: "Do not be afraid!" It is the most common one-liner in the Bible. Whenever an angel or God breaks into human life, the first words are invariably, "Do not be afraid." Why? Because people have always been afraid of God—and afraid of themselves, as a result. God was not usually "nice," and we were not too sure about ourselves either. (p. 3)

- How has God been likeable and/or to be feared in your life? In what ways do you fear and/or like God today?

- What do you fear about yourself? Do you notice any connections between how you view God and how you view yourself?

- When did you last tell someone not to be afraid? Take some time to remember as much as you can about the circumstances. Were the other(s) able to hear and accept your words? How did you feel?

5. *Lectio* Practice

After reading through these instructions, slowly read aloud the quotation below four times, following these instructions.

We don't really believe that God could naturally know and love what God has created, or that we could actually love (or even like!) God back. This is a fracture at the core of everything and creates the overwhelmingly shame- and guilt-based church and culture we have today in the West. (It was also at the heart of most of the European Reformations—on both sides.)

The amazing wonder of the biblical revelation, which I hope to make clear in this book, is that God is very different than we thought, and also much better than we feared. (pp. 4–5)

1. With the first reading of the quotation, allow yourself to *settle in* to the exercise and familiarize yourself with the words. Read the text out loud, very slowly and clearly. Pause for a breath or two before moving on.

2. For the second reading, *listen* from a centered heart space and notice any word or phrase that stands out to you.

3. After a few moments of silence, read the text a third time, *reflecting* on how this word or phrase is connected to your current

life experience. Take a minute to linger over this word or phrase and allow it to engage your body, heart, and awareness of the world around you.

You may want to speak a response aloud or write something in your journal.

4. For the final reading, *respond* with a prayer or expression of what you have experienced, inviting the infinite wisdom of God to support you in places of unknowing, confusion, desire, or hope.

6. Reflection

I know there were times when all of us have wished the Bible were some kind of "seven habits for highly effective people." *Just give us the right conclusions,* we've thought. (p. 6)

- In what ways have you wished the Bible was different than it is?
- Describe what you believe to be the purpose and goal of the Bible. How has this understanding changed over the course of your life?

7. Reflection

The genius of the biblical revelation is that it doesn't just give us the conclusions; it gives us both the process of getting there and the inner and outer authority to trust that process. To repeat, for the sake of emphasis: Life itself—and Scripture too—is always three steps forward and two steps backward. It gets the point and then loses it or doubts it. In that, the biblical text mirrors our own human consciousness and journey. (p. 6)

- Think back to a time when you felt your life journey was going "two steps backward." What stories or teachings from Scripture supported or challenged you during this time?

- Think back to a time when you felt your life journey was going "three steps forward." What stories or teachings from Scripture supported or challenged you during this time?

8. Contemplative Sit

Leading in with the quotation below, practice a contemplative sit. You may wish to set a timer or digital prayer bell for five, ten, or twenty minutes, so that you know when to finish. If engaging in a contemplative sit is new to you, begin with five minutes.

- Seat yourself in a quiet area.
- Ground yourself and allow your breathing to settle.
- Notice any tightness in your shoulders and neck and allow any tension in your muscles to relax.
- Allow your back to rest in an aligned, neutral position.
- Once you are settled, read the following passage aloud— this is the opening text for your sit:

When we get to the Risen Jesus, there is nothing to be afraid of in God. His very breath is identified with forgiveness and the Divine *Shalom* (see John 20:20–23). If the Risen Jesus is the final revelation of the nature of the heart of God, then suddenly we live in a safe and lovely universe. But it is not that God has changed, or that the Hebrew God is a different God than the God of Jesus. It is that we are growing up.... Stay with the text and with your inner life with God, and your capacity for God will increase and deepen. (p. 7)

- Continue your sit in silence—focusing on your breath, connecting with your body, or by practicing any other method with which you are familiar.

- Allow thoughts, feelings, and sensations to arise, exist, and then fall away while you keep your attention open and large, connecting to that much deeper consciousness.
- Remember, there is no goal. There is no right or wrong way—simply *be* present to what *is* in the moment.

Once finished, you may wish to journal your reflections on this experience.

9. Activity

Isn't it a consolation to know that life is not a straight line? Many of us wish it were—and have been told that it should be, but I haven't encountered a life yet that's a straight line to God, including Mother Teresa's! It's always getting the point and missing the point. It's God entering our lives and then us fighting it, avoiding it, running from it. There is the moment of divine communion or intimacy, and then the pullback that says, "That's too good to be true. I must be making it up." (p. 8)

- Gather a large piece of blank paper and some pens, markers, or crayons. Begin in an upper corner of the paper and write down your birth. Then chart your life journey along a line, letting it move up and down, back and forth and all around (and over?), the paper in whatever fashion makes sense to you. Make brief notes of those times when the line moves up or down, back or forth, to remind you of what led to those movements.
- When your charting of the journey feels complete enough for now, set your timer for five minutes, close your eyes or gaze at the floor in front of you, and rest in silence.
- When your timer goes off, look at the drawing you have made. What do you notice? What insights arise for you? What new connections might you see?

- Allow yourself to conclude with some time to journal about this experience.

10. Reflection

In this book, I'm going to name a healthy middle, a place between those alternating mediocrities. I'm going to bring some healthy cultural studies, psychology, and historical awareness to the task, but always point us toward an inner awareness of the Spirit that is guiding us right now. Such humility and trust will keep us humble before the text, and not so needy of quick conclusions. (p. 9)

- What feelings arose for you in reading this text?
- What experience do you have with bringing "healthy cultural studies, psychology, and historical awareness" to your reading of Scripture? What have been the results for you of such studies in the past?
- How quickly do you tend to jump to conclusions? What do you imagine it will be like to join Fr. Richard on this journey of "humility and trust"?

11. Reflection

Let me state it clearly: One great idea of the biblical revelation is that God is manifest in the ordinary, in the actual, in the daily, in the now, in the concrete incarnations of life. That's opposed to God holding out for the pure, the spiritual, the right idea or the ideal anything. This is why Jesus turns religion on its head! (p. 12)

- Recall a moment when you suddenly felt a sense of God's presence, or the holy, in an everyday moment. Allow yourself to remember as much as you can of where you were and what you saw, heard, smelled, possibly tasted, and touched.
- Can you articulate what "shifted" or "opened" in you to notice the manifestation of God or the holy?

- Reflect on how this type of experience is both similar and different from the religion you've been "taught."

12. Reflection

This journey is not about becoming spiritual beings nearly as much as it is about becoming human beings. The biblical revelation is saying that we are already spiritual beings; we just don't know it yet. The Bible tries to let us in on the secret by revealing God in the ordinary. That's why so much of the text seems so mundane, practical, specific, and, frankly, unspiritual! (pp. 12–13)

- How does it feel to have a spiritual teacher call the Bible "unspiritual"?
- Reread this text. What other feelings arise for you? Name them out loud or write them down in your journal.

13. Reflection

What we see built into the Hebrew Bible, and strongly expressed by Jesus and the prophets, is the *capacity for self-critical thinking. It is the first step beyond the dualistic mind and teaches us patience with ambiguity and mystery....*

   This is quite rare in the history of religion. This is the self-criticism necessary to keep religion from its natural tendency toward arrogant self-assurance. (p. 14)

- What is your experience with self-critical thinking? Does this idea feel "negative" or "positive" for you? Describe the thoughts and experiences that undergird those feelings.
- What is your experience with ambiguity and mystery? Do these ideas feel "negative" or "positive" for you? Describe the thoughts and experiences that undergird those feelings.

14. Reflection

Our temptation, now and always, is not to trust in God *but to trust in our faith tradition of trusting in God*. They are not the same thing! Often, our faith is in our tradition, in which we can talk about all our past saints and theologians who have trusted in God. That's a very clever way to avoid the experience itself, to avoid scary encounters with the living God, to avoid the ongoing Incarnation. (p. 15)

- When in your life have you experienced this temptation Fr. Richard describes? How has having faith in your tradition, instead of in your experience of God, impacted your life?

- Imagine yourself encountering "the living God." Notice what you are feeling as you imagine this, and how your body is responding to this imagined experience. What do your reactions have to teach you about your attitude toward God?

15. Reflection

Spend some time looking at the image of the Cosmic Egg on p. 17 of *Things Hidden* (and, if you need, reread the section on the Cosmic Egg on pp. 16–21). Then, reflect on the following questions.

- What do you notice about this image, as you sit with it in silence? What is it saying to you?

- In which dome(s) have you spent the most time, spiritually speaking, during your lifetime? What have been the blessings and the challenges of living out of the dome(s)?

- In which dome(s) have you spent the least time, spiritually speaking, during your lifetime? What might you have missed by avoiding the dome(s)?

- Which dome description is most surprising or revealing to you, and why?

16. Reflection

Suffering of some sort seems to be the only thing strong enough to destabilize our arrogance and our ignorance. I would define suffering very simply as "whenever we are not in control."

If religion cannot find a meaning for human suffering, humanity is in major trouble. All healthy religion shows us what to do with our pain. Great religion shows us what to do with the absurd, the tragic, the nonsensical, the unjust. *If we do not transform our pain, we will most assuredly transmit it.* (p. 22)

- Remember a time in your life when you transmitted your pain to someone else. What happened and what were the results? What did you learn about such experiences?
- How can your faith tradition help you find meaning for your suffering and pain? Imagine how that faith tradition could help you respond differently next time you are suffering.

17. Reflection

Biblical revelation is about transforming history and individuals so that we don't just keep handing on the pain to the next generation....

The biblical narrative is saying that there is coherence inside of the seeming incoherence of history. The Jewish people believed that our smaller stories have a Bigger Story holding them together. In this book, we're going to look for the interpretive clues for that Bigger Story. (p. 23)

- In what ways is this a new or unexpected perspective on the Bible for you?
- What is your gut-level response to approaching the Bible in this way?

18. Contemplative Sit

Leading in with the quotation below, practice a contemplative sit. You may wish to set a timer or digital prayer bell for five, ten, or twenty minutes, so that you know when to finish.

- Seat yourself in a quiet area.
- Ground yourself and allow your breathing to settle.
- Notice any tightness in your shoulders and neck and allow any tension in your muscles to relax.
- Allow your back to rest in an aligned, neutral position.
- Once you are settled, read the following passage aloud— this is the opening text for your sit:

The genius of the biblical revelation is that we will come to God through what I'm going to call "the actual," the here and now, or, quite simply, *what is*. The Bible moves us from sacred *place* (why the temple had to go) or sacred *action* (why the Law had to be relativized) or mental belief systems (why Jesus has no prerequisites in this regard) to time itself as sacred *time*. (p. 11)

- Continue your sit in silence—focusing on your breath, connecting with your body, or by practicing any other method with which you are familiar.
- Allow thoughts, feelings, and sensations to arise, exist, and then fall away while you keep your attention open and large, connecting to that much deeper consciousness.
- Remember, there is no goal. There is no right or wrong way—simply *be* present to what *is* in the moment.

Once finished, you may wish to journal your reflections on this experience.

CHAPTER TWO

Getting the "Who" Right

1. Contemplative Sit

Leading in with the quotation below, practice a contemplative sit. You may wish to set a timer or digital prayer bell for five, ten, or twenty minutes, so that you know when to finish.

- Seat yourself in a quiet area.
- Ground yourself and allow your breathing to settle.
- Notice any tightness in your shoulders and neck and allow any tension in your muscles to relax.
- Allow your back to rest in an aligned, neutral position.
- Once you are settled, read the following passage aloud— this is the opening text for your sit:

Our creation story declares that we were created in the very "image and likeness" of God, and out of generative love.... This starts us out on an absolutely positive and hopeful foundation, which cannot be overstated. (pp. 25-26)

- Continue your sit in silence—focusing on your breath, connecting with your body, or by practicing any other method with which you are familiar.
- Allow thoughts, feelings, and sensations to arise, exist, and then fall away while you keep your attention open and large, connecting to that much deeper consciousness.

- Remember, there is no goal. There is no right or wrong way—simply *be* present to what *is* in the moment.

Once finished, you may wish to journal your reflections on this experience.

2. Reflection

We have heard this phrase so often that we don't get the existential shock of what "created in the image and likeness of God" is saying about us. I always tell people that if we would just try to believe it, we could save ourselves ten thousand dollars in therapy! If this is true, it says that our family of origin is divine. Our core is original blessing, not original sin. (p. 26)

- What is your experience with the concept of original sin? How do Fr. Richard's words influence that understanding?
- In what ways is the concept of original blessing an existential shock for you—or not?
- How would you explain to someone else, in your own words, what it means to be "created in the image and likeness of God"?

3. Reflection

All of the Bible is trying to illustrate, through various stories, humanity's objective unity with God....

The great illusion that we must all overcome is the illusion of separateness. It is almost the only task of religion—to communicate, not worthiness, but union; to reconnect us to our original identity, "hidden with Christ in God" (Colossians 3:3). (pp. 26–27)

- Before you started reading *Things Hidden*, what did you think the Bible was trying to illustrate? How did that understanding impact your faith life and your view of God?

- Which stories in the Bible do you recall that illustrate humanity's unity with God? Which stories illustrate "the illusion of separateness"? If none come to mind, spend some time reading through the Book of Genesis with these questions in mind. What do you notice?

4. Reflection

The word *sin* has so many unhelpful connotations in most of our minds that it's very problematic today. For most of us, it does not connote a state of alienation or separateness. Instead, it connotes little naughty behaviors and personal moral unworthiness. But these are merely the symptoms and not the state itself! Disconnected people *will* do stupid things. (p. 27)

- What is your personal history with the word *sin*? How has it changed over time? How does your current understanding of sin relate to what Fr. Richard says here?
- What is your response to Fr. Richard's statement that "Disconnected people *will* do stupid things"? What lies at the root of that response?

5. Reflection

It is not that *if* I am moral, *then* I will be loved by God, but rather that I must first come to experience God's love, and then I will—almost naturally—be moral. (p. 28)

- What is your spontaneous, gut-level response to these words? Does this seem too easy, or too hard? Too unbelievable, or too ordinary?
- What, if anything, holds you back from believing in God's love?

- Speak this quotation out loud several times, listening to the words as you speak them. What do you notice?

6. Reflection

God does not change in the text, but we do. The written words are inspired precisely insofar as they inspire and change *us*! Here, I am using the literal meaning of the word *inspire*—to "breathe into us" a Larger Life. If the written words do not accomplish that, then they are not at all "inspired"—at least for us. (p. 29)

- Describe your perspective on the idea that the Scriptures are "inspired." How is this similar or different from Fr. Richard's perspective? What do the differences reveal to you?
- When has the Bible inspired you? What happened, and how did you respond? What new outlook or belief unfolded from that event?

7. Reflection

God is not afraid of mistakes, it seems. God knows that God can turn everything around—into good. There are no dead ends in the economy of grace. (p. 29)

- When have you made mistakes? How has God turned those events around, and brought good out of them? What did you learn, and how did you grow, through that process?
- How would you describe "the economy of grace" to someone unfamiliar with Christianity?

8. *Lectio* Practice

God's main problem is how to give away God! But God has great difficulty doing this. You'd think everybody would want God, but the common response is something like this: "Lord, I am not worthy. I would rather

> have religion and morality, which give me the impression that I can win
> a cosmic contest by my own efforts." (p. 30)

Slowly read aloud the quotation above four times, following these instructions.

1. With the first reading of the quotation text, allow yourself to *settle in* to the exercise and familiarize yourself with the words. Read the text out loud, very slowly and clearly. Pause for a breath or two before moving on.

2. For the second reading, *listen* from a centered heart space and notice any word or phrase that stands out to you.

3. After a few moments of silence, read the text a third time, *reflecting* on how this word or phrase is connected to your current life experience. Take a minute to linger over this word or phrase and allow it to engage your body, heart, and awareness of the world around you.

   You may want to speak a response aloud or write something in your journal.

4. For the final reading, *respond* with a prayer or expression of what you have experienced, inviting the infinite wisdom of God to support you in places of unknowing, confusion, desire, or hope.

9. Reflection

> The first act of divine revelation is creation itself. I call nature the very first Bible, which was written approximately fourteen billion years before the Bible of words. God initially speaks through *what is*. (p. 30)

- How does it feel to have Fr. Richard name nature as "the very first Bible"? In what ways do you welcome and/or resist this idea?

- Describe what you have learned from the Scripture of creation over the course of your life. In what ways are those lessons different from the ones you learned from the Bible?

10. Reflection

Unfortunately, the word *sin* in our vocabulary has come to imply culpability or personal fault, and that is not at all what the doctrine meant to convey. In fact, the precise meaning of original sin is that we are *not* culpable for it, but we must recognize that a wound is there, and that *all* people share in it.

In that sense, it should make us much more patient and empathetic with reality. It names our inner conflict, so we will not be surprised or scandalized when it shows itself. The doctrine of original sin puts humanity on an honest and compassionate stage, right at the beginning.

The doctrine of original sin is actually a consolation, because if you know you are a mixed blessing, that you are filled with contradictions, a mystery to yourself, then you won't pretend that you can totally eliminate all that you consider unworthy of yourself. (pp. 32–33)

- Write down the understanding of "original sin" that you had before beginning to read *Things Hidden*.

- What is it like for you to read that the "doctrine of original sin is actually a consolation"? What is stirred up for you, or set free, or confounded?

- What do you notice in comparing your initial understanding of "original sin" with what Fr. Richard describes here? In what ways would you like to amend your written description of original sin?

11. Reflection

God isn't looking for slaves, workers, or contestants to play the game or jump through hoops correctly. God is simply looking for images. God wants images of God to walk around the earth! ...

This is amazing. It's as if God is saying, "All I want are some living icons out there who will communicate who I am, what I'm about, and what is happening in me." (p. 34)

- What is your understanding of the reason God created human beings? Where does that understanding come from and how has it influenced your life?
- How does it feel for you to read that God wants you to be a "living icon" rather than "slave, worker, or contestant"? How would believing you are a living icon change the way you live your life?
- As a living icon, how would you describe God? How would you reveal what God is doing in your life, in your community, and in the world today?

12. Reflection

God tells Noah to bring into the ark all the opposites: the wild and the domestic, the crawling and the flying, the clean and the unclean, the male and the female of each animal (Genesis 7:2–15).

That, in itself, is understandable. But then God does a most amazing thing. God locks them together inside the ark (Genesis 7:16). Most people never note that God actually closed them in! God puts all the natural animosities, all the opposites, together, and holds them together in one place. I used to think it was about *balancing* all the opposites within me, but slowly I have learned that it is actually "holding" things *unreconciled* that teaches us—leaving them partly unresolved and without perfect closure or explanation. How to live in hope has not been taught well to Christians. The ego always wants to settle the dust quickly and have immediate answers. But Paul rightly writes, "In hope we are saved, yet hope is not hope if its object is seen" (Romans 8:24). (p. 35)

- When have you been compelled to live in hope during your life? How did that impact your understanding of yourself, of God, and of the nature of hope?
- How do you currently handle unreconciled and unresolved aspects of your life? What do you think Fr. Richard would advise you, based on this reading?
- What changes do you think God would want you to make in your attitude toward what is unreconciled in your life?

13. Reflection

I think forgiveness is the only event in which we simultaneously experience three great graces: God's unmerited goodness, the deeper goodness of the one we have forgiven, and the experience of our own gratuitous goodness. That's the payoff. This makes the mystery of forgiveness an incomparable tool of salvation. (p. 36)

- What is it like for you to read that "forgiveness [is] an incomparable tool of salvation"? How does it influence your understanding of both forgiveness and salvation?
- What feelings arise in you when you read that both you and the one you must forgive are good in God's eyes? Is it harder to believe that you or the other person is good, and why?

14. Contemplative Sit

Leading in with the quotation below, practice a contemplative sit. You may wish to set a timer or digital prayer bell for five, ten, or twenty minutes, so that you know when to finish.

- Seat yourself in a quiet area.
- Ground yourself and allow your breathing to settle.
- Notice any tightness in your shoulders and neck and allow any tension in your muscles to relax.
- Allow your back to rest in an aligned, neutral position.
- Once you are settled, read the following passage aloud—this is the opening text for your sit:

There is really nothing else quite like [forgiveness] for inner transformation, which is why all spiritual teachers insist upon it, both in the giving and the receiving. (p. 36)

- Continue your sit in silence—focusing on your breath, connecting with your body, or by practicing any other method with which you are familiar.
- Allow thoughts, feelings, and sensations to arise, exist, and then fall away while you keep your attention open and large, connecting to that much deeper consciousness.
- Remember, there is no goal. There is no right or wrong way—simply *be* present to what *is* in the moment.

Once finished, you may wish to journal your reflections on this experience.

15. Reflection

Some would think that is the whole meaning of Christianity: to be able to decide who's going to heaven and who isn't. This is much more a search for control than it is a search for truth, love, or God. It has to do with ego, which needs to pigeonhole everything to give itself that sense of "I know" and "I am in control of the data."...

I guess God knew that such would be the direction that religion would take. So, God said, "Don't do it. Don't eat of the tree of the knowledge of good and evil." God is trying to keep us from a lust for certitude, an undue need for explanation, resolution, and answers. Frankly, these make biblical faith impossible.

The major heresy of the Western churches is that they have largely turned around the very meaning of faith—not knowing and not needing to know—into its exact opposite: *demanding to know and insisting that we do know!* (p. 37)

- In what ways do you seek to control your own life and the lives of others? What would it take for you to hold this need to control more loosely, or to even let it go at times? What would it mean to do so?
- What is your relationship with knowledge? How do you feel about not knowing, and mystery? What lies at the root of those feelings?

16. Reflection

The Fall is not simply something that happened to Adam and Eve in one historical moment. It's something that happens in all moments and all lives. It must happen and will happen to all of us. In fact, as the English mystic Julian of Norwich (1342–1416) said, "First the fall, and then the recovery from the fall, and both are the mercy of God." It is in falling down that we learn almost everything that matters spiritually. (pp. 38–39)

- What have you been taught about "the Fall"? What does it mean to you that humans are "fallen"? In what ways does Fr. Richard's teaching challenge or confirm your understanding of the Fall and experience of being fallen?
- What would it take for you to believe that God's mercy is in both fall and recovery? What beliefs and understandings

would have to change for you to accept and embrace this idea?

17. Reflection

The perfect metaphor for this new split universe, this intense awareness of themselves as separate and cut off, is that "they realized they were naked" (3:7). Today, we would probably call it primal shame. Every human being seems to have it in some form: that deep sense of being inadequate, insecure, separate, judged, and apart. It is almost the human condition, yet it takes a thousand disguises. It creates the yearning for divine re-communion. (p. 40)

- How would you describe the impact of "primal shame" in your life? What words would you use? What experiences would illustrate it?
- What is the impact on you of learning that this primal shame is about "yearning for divine re-communion"? How does it change your perspective on these elements of your life?
- How does reading this impact your perspective on the people around you?

18. Reflection and Activity

God takes away the shame we have *by giving us back to ourselves*—by giving us God! It doesn't get any better than that. Human love does the same thing. When someone else loves us, they give us not just themselves, but, for some reason, they give us back our own self, but now a truer and better self. This dance between the Lover and the beloved is the psychology of the whole Bible. (pp. 41–42)

- What has human love taught you about God's love?
- When and how have you lived out this "dance" Fr. Richard describes, even if just for a few moments?

- How does it feel to have God described as Lover, and yourself as beloved? What would it take for you to be able to embrace this description wholeheartedly?

- Find or clear a safe place where you can move around a little without tripping over something or stubbing your toes. It might be outdoors in a field, or in a basement room, or the back of a church sanctuary or meeting hall. Play some gentle, loving music if you can, wrap your arms around yourself, and begin to gently move side to side. (If standing and moving is difficult, do this while seated in a chair.) Close your eyes if that feels safe, or let your gaze go soft. Imagine that the arms wrapping you round are the arms of a loving God. Slowly allow yourself to be drawn into the dance. Let go and let God lead the movements. Notice how your movements change. Feel yourself as beloved. Dance in whatever way feels best, for as long as you need to. When you are finished, thank God for the dance.

You may wish to reflect on the dance experience in your journal.

19. Reflection

Being chosen doesn't mean that God likes one [person] more than the other, or that some are better than others. Usually, in fact, they are quite flawed, or at least ordinary, people, so it is clear that their power is not their own. As Paul will put it, "If anyone wants to boast, they can only boast about the Lord" (1 Corinthians 1:31). (p. 43)

- How have you viewed and responded to people that you think are chosen by God? How would that perspective shift if you came to believe that they are "ordinary" just like you?

- Who do you know who "can only boast about the Lord"? How do you respond to such people? What have you learned from them?
- Would you want to be chosen by God? Why or why not?

20. Reflection

If we do not understand election as *inclusive* election (chosenness is for the sake of communicating the same to others), religion almost always becomes an exclusionary system against the "non-elect," "unworthy," or "impure." It becomes "my belonging system" instead of any good news for the world, which is exactly what Jesus did *not* do. (p. 44)

- What "belonging systems" have you joined (or been born into) in your life? What did you get out of belonging? How did belonging make you feel, about yourself and about others?
- When have you considered someone else as "unworthy" or "impure"? Why? What did you gain, and/or lose, from feeling that way?

21. Activity

The first bookmark is the symbol of God's constant and gracious invitation to union, God flowing out toward us, God choosing us before we ever choose back. The code word for that is *water*.

Water is almost always an invitation to that first, subtle religious experience, when the desire just laps up against us and our mind and heart are opened for the first time. It's the first gnawing, inviting sense that there's something more. (pp. 45–46)

- Slowly pour yourself a full glass of water. Listen to the sound of the water flowing into the glass.

- Notice the sensations in your mouth as the glass fills. Is your mouth dry? Does saliva flow in anticipation of receiving water? Do you have a sense of thirst?
- Hold the full glass in your hand and feel its heaviness. See the clarity of the water. Imagine being in the desert with the ancient Israelites, thirsting for water and for a place to call home.
- Close your eyes and ask yourself what you are thirsting for at this time in your life. Listen for your soul's response.
- Open your eyes, bring the glass to your lips, and let the water wet your lips. Breathe through your nose. Then open your lips and let some water flow into your mouth. How does your body respond?
- Swallow, and feel the water flow down your throat and into your belly. How does your body respond to the inflow of this water?
- Gradually and mindfully drink as much of the water as you wish. Notice when your body says you have enough for now.
- Give thanks to God for the gift of water, and the quenching of your physical and spiritual thirsts.

You may wish to reflect in your journal following this exercise.

22. Reflection

The Hebrew Scriptures are filled with images of blood sacrifice. There are the frequent burnt offerings, the paschal lamb that has to be killed, and, of course, the many temple sacrifices. By the time of Jesus, 90 percent of the economy of the city of Jerusalem was tied up in the hauling, penning, feeding, and killing of sacrificial animals, and then the hauling of dead carcasses back out of the temple....

This was never revealed in any detail in our anesthetized Bible-history books because it was too unbelievable. But to be a priest or Levite was also to be a butcher. A demanding or distant God always needs to be placated with blood, it seems....

Suffice it to say that we probably could not even imagine or picture *God loving us* without the spilling of blood on God's part (that's how deep the archetypal symbolism flows). As the dualistic mind tends to do, we made the Crucifixion into a tit-for-tat event instead of a revelation of the eternal nature of the heart of God, flowing toward us as water and blood (see John 19:34). (p. 47)

- How does your gut respond to reading these words about worship in the Jerusalem temple? What do your mind and your heart want to do with this information?
- Imagine arriving to worship at the temple in Jesus's day. What would you hear? What would you see? What would you smell? How does all this impact your understanding of and relationship with God? How does it modify your concept of worship?
- How does this discussion of blood impact your understanding of and feelings about Jesus's crucifixion?

23. Reflection

[In Jesus,] God [is] spilling God's blood to get to us, after millennia of humanity spilling its blood to get to God! (p. 48)

- What is your response to this declaration? What views and assumptions influence your response?
- Write a letter to Jesus in which you share your thoughts and feelings about the crucifixion in light of Fr. Richard's declaration.

24. Reflection

Food—and bread in particular—seems to be used to symbolize fullness and satisfaction in God. It's God feeding us, rather than we being food for God. It's God caring even about our very mundane and immediate needs for "daily bread." God is offering us abundance rather than mere fear-based, subsistence religion. (p. 49)

- In what ways have you experienced "fear-based, subsistence religion"? How did it impact your understanding of and openness to God?

- What does it mean for you that God wants to give you an abundance of "daily bread"? How does this describe the God you think you know—or not? What would need to change for you to embrace this idea fully?

- When in your life have you experienced God's abundance? What made you think (or allowed you to believe) God was the source?

25. Reflection

What the biblical revelation is achieving is basically a very different consciousness, a recreated self, an "identity transplant"—just as today we talk about kidney and heart transplants. The text is inviting us slowly, little by little, into a very, very different sense of who we are.

We are not our own! Or, as I would tell the men at the initiation rites, "Your life is not about you." We move from the lesser self to the Great Self. (p. 50)

- This chapter is full of opportunities to imagine an "identity transplant." Sit in silence and let your mind range back over all that has been covered. What stands out for you, and why?

- What is your gut-level response to this statement: "Your life is not about you"? What questions does it raise for you? What emotional response arises within you?
- What changes would be required in your life for you to begin to live for God rather than for yourself?

26. Contemplative Sit

Leading in with the quotation below, practice a contemplative sit. You may wish to set a timer or digital prayer bell for five, ten, or twenty minutes, so that you know when to finish. If engaging in a contemplative sit is new to you, begin with five minutes.

- Seat yourself in a quiet area.
- Ground yourself and allow your breathing to settle.
- Notice any tightness in your shoulders and neck and allow any tension in your muscles to relax.
- Allow your back to rest in an aligned, neutral position.
- Once you are settled, read the following passage aloud— this is the opening text for your sit:

We realize that we are a mere drop in a Bigger Ocean, and what's happening in the ocean is happening in us. (p. 50)

- Continue your sit in silence—focusing on your breath, connecting with your body, or by practicing any other method with which you are familiar.
- Allow thoughts, feelings, and sensations to arise, exist, and then fall away while you keep your attention open and large, connecting to that much deeper consciousness.
- Remember, there is no goal. There is no right or wrong way—simply *be* present to what *is* in the moment.

Once finished, you may wish to journal your reflections on this experience.

CHAPTER THREE

People Who Have Faces

1. Contemplative Sit

Leading in with the quotation below, practice a contemplative sit. You may wish to set a timer or digital prayer bell for five, ten, or twenty minutes, so that you know when to finish.

- Seat yourself in a quiet area.
- Ground yourself and allow your breathing to settle.
- Notice any tightness in your shoulders and neck and allow any tension in your muscles to relax.
- Allow your back to rest in an aligned, neutral position.
- Once you are settled, read the following passage aloud— this is the opening text for your sit:

God does not settle for mandated or fear-based relationships, but rather desires willing and free relationships with "friends." (p. 53)

- Continue your sit in silence—focusing on your breath, connecting with your body, or by practicing any other method with which you are familiar.
- Allow thoughts, feelings, and sensations to arise, exist, and then fall away while you keep your attention open and large, connecting to that much deeper consciousness.
- Remember, there is no goal. There is no right or wrong way—simply *be* present to what *is* in the moment.

Once finished, you may wish to journal your reflections on this experience.

2. Reflection

God is creating, quite literally, some friends for Godself! Jesus became the full representation of one who accepted and lived that friendship. In fact, he never seemed to doubt it. That must be at the core of our imitation of Jesus. (p. 53)

- Write down your definition of friendship. Can you imagine having this kind of relationship with God? What attitudes or perspectives would need to change for you to accept such a friendship?
- Think back on the story of Jesus in the Gospels. What aspects of friendship come to mind in your memories of Jesus's relationship with God?
- If God desires friends, how does this change your outlook on your fellow creatures?

3. Reflection

In calling forth such freedom and consciousness, and even love, in humanity, God is actually making possible a certain kind of equality between Divinity and humanity, as strange and impossible as that might sound. (p. 54)

- What arose in your mind and heart as you read these words? Do you resist or embrace this idea of equality, and why?
- How have you defined "freedom" in your life? In what ways does this paragraph shift your understanding of the term?
- If God intends "equality between Divinity and humanity," how does this impact your relationships with your fellow creatures?

4. Reflection

One way to read the entire Bible is to note the gradual unveiling of our faces, the steady creating of personhood from infancy to teenage love, to infatuation, to adult communion. (p. 54)

- How have you read the Bible in the past? What changes in your understanding of the Bible as a whole when you think about it as "the gradual unveiling of our faces"?

- What feelings arise for you when Fr. Richard uses words like "teenage love" and "infatuation" to describe elements of the Bible? Does this make the Bible more or less appealing to you, and why?

- What does the phrase "creating of personhood" mean to you?

5. Reflection

The Judeo-Christian tradition really nurtured and brought forth the idea of the individual that was so prevalent among the ancient Greeks. That's probably why we have this strong sense of individuality in the West, which we often think of in negative terms. But there's a very positive sense to it too. Humanity had to be pulled out of tribalism, collectivism, and groupthink, which is where human consciousness started. (p. 54)

- What is your understanding of and perspective on individuality? What has been negative and what has been positive about the Western focus on the individual, beyond what Fr. Richard describes here?

- What is your understanding of and perspective on community? What has been negative and what has been positive about the Western understanding of community?

6. Reflection

Non-Dual Consciousness or "the unitive way"...is utterly mysterious and unknown to people in the first stage, and still rather scary and threatening to people in the second stage. *If we are not trained in a trust of mystery and some degree of tolerance for ambiguity, we will not proceed very far on the spiritual journey. In fact, we will often run back to stage one when the going gets rough in stage two.* (p. 55)

- Describe what it would mean to have "a trust of mystery." What internal shifts would need to happen for this to be true of you?

- Recall a time when the going got "rough" and you embraced a tribal, collective, "Simple Consciousness"? Describe what happened, how you felt, and what you thought at that time. What has changed in you since that time? What is your viewpoint on that period of your life now?

7. *Lectio* Practice

Love is the true goal, but faith is the process of getting there, and hope is the willingness to live without resolution or closure. They are indeed, "the three things that last." (p. 55)

Slowly read aloud the quotation above four times, following these instructions.

1. With the first reading of the text, allow yourself to *settle in* to the exercise and familiarize yourself with the words. Read the text out loud, very slowly and clearly. Pause for a breath or two before moving on.

2. For the second reading, *listen* from a centered heart space and notice any word or phrase that stands out to you.

3. After a few moments of silence, read the text a third time, *reflecting* on how this word or phrase is connected to your current life experience. Take a minute to linger over this word or phrase and allow it to engage your body, heart, and awareness of the world around you.

You may want to speak a response aloud or write something in your journal.

4. For the final reading, *respond* with a prayer or expression of what you have experienced, inviting the infinite wisdom of God to support you in places of unknowing, confusion, desire, or hope.

8. Reflection

It seems we all fear and avoid intimacy. It is too powerful and demands that we also "have faces"—that is, *self-confidence, identity, dignity, and a certain courage to accept our own unique face.* Then, even worse, it demands that, once we have it, we be willing to give it away to another. (p. 56)

- What is your experience with intimacy? Remembering that God desires our friendship, what feelings arise when you consider being intimate with God?
- How would you assess your levels of self-confidence, identity, and dignity? What would you like to change in each of these areas? What would it take to accept yourself, as you are right now, knowing that you can continue to grow and change in the future?
- What do you think Fr. Richard means when he writes that we must "be willing to give [our unique face] away to another"? How would you imagine that happening?

9. Reflection

It seems the experience of specialness is almost too awesome to be carried by an individual. We will either disbelieve it or abuse it, either by ego deflation or ego inflation, self-hatred or conceit. We see, even now, how difficult it is for a person to stand before the face of God in that perfect balance between humility and dignity. (p. 56)

- Is your tendency toward ego deflation or ego inflation? What self-understanding and past experiences undergird and reinforce that tendency?
- How would you imagine being able to move toward a middle road between self-hatred and conceit? What practices or helpful self-talk could support such an endeavor?

10. Reflection

We could say, "In the beginning is the relationship," like the Trinity itself, yet the relationship is between the group and Yahweh. How we relate to God always reveals how we will relate to people, and how we relate to people is an almost infallible indicator of how we relate to God and let God relate to us. The whole Bible is a school of relationship, revealing both its best qualities and its worst. (p. 57)

- Think about the groups you belong to, including and beyond any church community. How would you describe the relationships between people and between the group and God? Where do you see the relational connections Fr. Richard describes?
- What has the Bible taught you about human relationships? Make a list of "both its best qualities and its worst." Read through the list and journal about what you notice.

11. Reflection

The Bible is slowly making us capable of entering into that co-inherence; it is giving us a face capable of receiving divine dignity, and even daring to think that we could love God back—and that God would care!

We are gradually being drawn inside the very mystery of Divine sharing. Teresa of Ávila described it as "the interior castle." John's whole Gospel could be seen as one great meditation on that momentous realization, especially chapters 13-17, where John is almost drunk with inner realizations of union and divine election. (p. 57)

- What feelings arise when you read that the Bible "is giving us a face capable of receiving divine dignity"? What is your response to this "momentous realization"?
- Can you believe and accept the idea that God cares? How would your life change if you embraced this idea in every moment?
- Write down your understanding of union with God. What would be possible, and what would become impossible, if you could have union with God?

12. Contemplative Sit

Leading in with the quotation below, practice a contemplative sit. You may wish to set a timer or digital prayer bell for five, ten, or twenty minutes, so that you know when to finish.

- Seat yourself in a quiet area.
- Ground yourself and allow your breathing to settle.
- Notice any tightness in your shoulders and neck and allow any tension in your muscles to relax.
- Allow your back to rest in an aligned, neutral position.

Once you are settled, read the following passage aloud—this is the opening text for your sit:

This new science, which arose in Einstein's footsteps, sees no such thing in the whole universe as autonomy. It seems that any kind of autonomy or self-sufficiency is a total illusion. (pp. 57–58)

- Continue your sit in silence—focusing on your breath, connecting with your body, or by practicing any other method with which you are familiar.
- Allow thoughts, feelings, and sensations to arise, exist, and then fall away while you keep your attention open and large, connecting to that much deeper consciousness.
- Remember, there is no goal. There is no right or wrong way—simply *be* present to what *is* in the moment.

Once finished, you may wish to journal your reflections on this experience.

13. *Lectio* Practice

In terms of our humanity, without *some significant other* naming us, we have a very fragile sense of ourselves. "Many gods before us" is like a state of sexual promiscuity; the person remains scattered, dissipated, without focus, and like a "reed shaking in the wind" (see Matthew 11:7). This is particularly true of young people, although it's true for most people in the secular West today. *Without a significant other, who is also The Significant Other, we are burdened with being our own center and circumference.* (p. 59)

Slowly read aloud the quotation above four times, following these instructions.

1. With the first reading of the text, allow yourself to *settle in* to the exercise and familiarize yourself with the words. Read the text out loud, very slowly and clearly. Pause for a breath or two before moving on.

2. For the second reading, *listen* from a centered heart space and notice any word or phrase that stands out to you.

3. After a few moments of silence, read the text a third time, *reflecting* on how this word or phrase is connected to your current life experience. Take a minute to linger over this word or phrase and allow it to engage your body, heart, and awareness of the world around you.

You may want to speak a response aloud or write something in your journal.

4. For the final reading, *respond* with a prayer or expression of what you have experienced, inviting the infinite wisdom of God to support you in places of unknowing, confusion, desire, or hope.

14. Reflection

I would note that when I was a nineteen-year-old Franciscan novice, most of my classmates and I were very happy people, joking and peaceful most of the time. Our little world was whittled down to absolute essentials, and inside of that we were quite content. That is the value of stage one, simple consciousness, and why so many want to stay there. The trouble is that it is not yet integrated, mature, or even highly conscious. Most of us were living on the cruise control of obeying laws and our positive self-image, which had yet to be tried. It was the best kind of beginning. (p. 60)

- Think about your own upbringing and young adulthood. In what ways was it similar to Fr. Richard's? In what ways was it different?
- Look back at the chart of your life's journey that you created in Activity 9 of Chapter One. Notice those times when you were living in that "stage one, simple consciousness."

What adjectives would you use to describe your life during those times?

- Think of times in your life when you wanted to stay in or return to such "simple" times. What drew or pulled you away? What have been the graces and griefs of leaving such simple times behind?

15. Reflection

One way to think of "being possessed" is when there is *an unhealthy other* who is defining us, and defining us poorly. It's when a negative projection or agenda has captured us and we have internalized it, either consciously or unconsciously. (p. 60)

- What is your gut-level response to this definition of possession? What appeals to you about it? What do you instinctively want to reject, and why?
- What would change in your life if this was your definition of possession?
- Remember a time in your life when you were "possessed" in the way Fr. Richard describes. What poor and negative definitions and agendas influenced you?
- When and how have you been able to move beyond these unhealthy projections and agendas?

16. Reflection

When a holy person, or a totally accepting person, becomes your chosen and choosing mirror, you are, in fact, healed! I hope it does not sound too presumptuous, but I think I have exorcised a good number of people in my life—and it was because *they* had the trust and the humility to let me mirror them positively and replace the old mirror of their abusive dad, their toxic church, or their racist neighborhood. (p. 61)

- Who have been the "holy" or "totally accepting" people who took on the role of healing mirrors in your life? In what ways did they do this?

- When have you been a healing mirror for someone else? What happened, and how did they respond? What was the impact on your life?

- In what ways can you intentionally seek to live as a healing mirror for those around you?

17. Reflection

The Bible is always calling forth a positive "Thou" to which God can be an "I," which wonderfully takes away our own negative "I." That is really the heart of the matter. The I-Thou language of Martin Buber is a way of speaking of the Lover-Beloved relationship, and it is qualitatively quite different than the I-It relationship, where everything is functional, impersonal, and earned. Sin could almost be defined as living our whole life inside of I-It and never experiencing the I-Thou relationship of a Beloved. (p. 61)

- How would you describe the difference between I-Thou and I-It in your own words? What experience from your life would you use to illustrate the difference?

- What is your response to Fr. Richard's definition of sin here? In what ways does it affirm and/or contradict your current understanding of sin?

- How does it feel to read our relationship with God being described as "Lover-Beloved"? What attracts you in that concept, and why? What frightens you or repels you, and why?

18. Reflection

Most of us grew up thinking that mysteries were things we could not understand, so we should not try. But that's not the traditional or true meaning of the word. Mystery is not something that we cannot understand, but rather something that is *endlessly understandable!* It is multilayered and pregnant with meaning and never totally admits to closure or resolution. (pp. 62–63)

- In what ways do you use the word *mystery* in your life? How are those uses different from what Fr. Richard describes here?
- How important are closure and resolution for you? What would it mean to accept that you can "never totally" understand something as important as an element of your faith?

19. Reflection

Christians speak of the "paschal mystery," the process of loss and renewal that was lived and personified in the death and raising up of Jesus. We can affirm that belief in ritual and song, as we do in the Eucharist, but until people have lost their foundation and ground, and then experienced God upholding them so that they come out even more alive on the other side, the expression "paschal mystery" is little understood and not essentially transformative.

Paschal mystery is a doctrine to which Christians would probably intellectually assent, but it is not yet the very cornerstone of their life philosophy. That is the difference between belief systems and living faith. *We move from one to the other only through encounter, surrender, trust, and an inner experience of presence and power.* (pp. 63–64)

- When have you lost your "foundation and ground"? Were you aware of God upholding you at the time, later, or not at all? How does your memory of that experience influence your understanding of the "paschal mystery"?

- How are you aware of God upholding you now?
- In what areas of your life do you have "belief systems"? In what areas of your life do you have a "living faith"? How would you describe the difference in your own words?

20. Reflection

The really great truths, like love and inner freedom, are not fully conceptual, and they can never be understood by reason alone. They can never be "proven" to others, whether you have a PhD or even five degrees in theology. They are known holistically—that is, when *all* of you is there! (This is no easy task, by the way.) (p. 64)

- When have you tried to prove a great truth to another person? What happened? How did you feel about that discussion, at the time and afterward?
- When have others tried to prove something to you? What happened? How did you feel about that discussion, at the time and afterward?
- What, if anything, do you know "holistically"? How might you bring more of yourself to something you're working to understand?

21. Contemplative Sit

Leading in with the quotation below, practice a contemplative sit. You may wish to set a timer or digital prayer bell for five, ten, or twenty minutes, so that you know when to finish.

- Seat yourself in a quiet area.
- Ground yourself and allow your breathing to settle.
- Notice any tightness in your shoulders and neck and allow any tension in your muscles to relax.

- Allow your back to rest in an aligned, neutral position.
- Once you are settled, read the following passage aloud—this is the opening text for your sit:

Biblical rightness is primarily right relationship! (p. 64)

- Continue your sit in silence—focusing on your breath, connecting with your body, or by practicing any other method with which you are familiar.
- Allow thoughts, feelings, and sensations to arise, exist, and then fall away while you keep your attention open and large, connecting to that much deeper consciousness.
- Remember, there is no goal. There is no right or wrong way—simply *be* present to what *is* in the moment.

Once finished, you may wish to journal your reflections on this experience.

22. Reflection

The mystery of presence is *that encounter wherein the self-disclosure of one evokes a deeper life in the other*. There is nothing we need to "think" or understand to be present; it is all about giving and receiving, right now, and it is not done in the mind. It is actually *a transference and sharing of Being*, and will be experienced as grace, gratuity, and inner groundedness. (p. 65)

- What does "Being" mean to you? How would you explain it to another Christian?
- When have you experienced "the mystery of presence" that Fr. Richard describes? Spend some time writing down everything you can remember about it, including not just

what happened, but also what you felt and thought then, and what you feel and think about it now.

- What level of vulnerability would be required for such self-disclosure and the receiving of a "deeper life"? What would need to change in you for this to be possible for you?

- Fr. Richard writes that "we really are socially contagious human beings, but we settle for 'human doings'" (p. 65). How would you describe the difference?

23. Reflection and Activity

The lover can say, "It's as if I never knew myself until you knew me," or "It's as if I never could accept myself until you accepted me." That's how fragile we are and how needy we are of another's love and affirmation. Thus, Jesus said, "When you forgive others, they are unbound, and those you don't forgive, you keep them bound up" (John 20:23). (p. 66)

- Do you consider yourself fragile? Do you need others' love and affirmation? How does it feel to have Fr. Richard describe all of us this way?

- When have you allowed someone else to know and accept you in love? How did that experience change your life?

- Spend some time writing down the names of those people in your life that you have not been able to forgive. Do you feel "bound up" by that unforgiveness? How might they also be "bound up" in your unforgiveness? Are there any people on the list that you might be ready to forgive? How could you do that? Will you make a commitment to forgive at least one person on your list before one week has passed? How does it feel to make that commitment? Spend some time reflecting on all this in your journal.

24. *Lectio* Practice

> To have naked interface with the Ultimate Other is to know ourselves in our truest and deepest being. When we allow ourselves to be perfectly received, totally gazed upon by the One who knows everything and receives everything, we are indestructible.
>
> If we can learn how to receive the perfect gaze of the Other, to be mirrored by the Other, then the voices of the human crowd, even negative ones, have little power to hurt us. (p. 66)

Slowly read aloud the quotation above four times, following these instructions.

1. With the first reading of the text, allow yourself to *settle in* to the exercise and familiarize yourself with the words. Read the text out loud, very slowly and clearly. Pause for a breath or two before moving on.

2. For the second reading, *listen* from a centered heart space and notice any word or phrase that stands out to you.

3. After a few moments of silence, read the text a third time, *reflecting* on how this word or phrase is connected to your current life experience. Take a minute to linger over this word or phrase and allow it to engage your body, heart, and awareness of the world around you.

You may want to speak a response aloud or write something in your journal.

4. For the final reading, *respond* with a prayer or expression of what you have experienced, inviting the infinite wisdom of God to support you in places of unknowing, confusion, desire, or hope.

25. Reflection

Standing humbly before God's gaze not only unites the psyche, but it also does the very thing that I know when I teach contemplative prayer: It unifies desire. It frees us from what Henri de Lubac (1896–1991) called the *vertigo of imagination*. It's the whirlpool of imagination: looking here, there, and everywhere. Standing before *one, accepting* God literally allows us to be composed and gathered into one place. We *can* be in one place. We *can* be here, now. We stop always looking over there for tomorrow's happiness. (p. 67)

- What is your response to this description of contemplative prayer? How could it impact your own contemplative prayer practice? If you don't practice contemplative prayer, does it encourage you to begin, or not, and why?
- Imagine yourself standing in the center of that "whirlpool of imagination." What swirls around you? Look up and see God gazing lovingly at you. What do you feel? What happens? What shifts in your body, mind, and heart?

26. Reflection

My definition of a Christian might not seem like one at all: *A true Christian is invariably someone who has met a true Christian.* I even wonder if, in a sense, that is not the real meaning of the passing on of "apostolic succession." The mystery of the Risen Christ is passed on by mutual presence and communion. (p. 68)

It doesn't have to do with being perfect. It has to do with staying in relationship, "hanging in there," holding onto union as tightly as God holds onto us. The one who knows all and receives all, as a mirror does, has no trouble forgiving all. It's not a matter of being correct, but of being connected. (p. 69)

- Are you "a true Christian," according to Fr. Richard's definition? When and how did it happen? If you don't believe you have met "a true Christian," how would you describe the differences between his description and your most holy interpersonal experiences?
- Which is more difficult: striving for perfection or staying connected in relationship? Why?
- How might you pass on "apostolic succession" in this way? How can you be more mutually present and mirroring to people in your life? Can you make a commitment to do this in the days ahead?

27. Reflection

Abstractions offer the ego lots of payoffs: We can remain seemingly in control; we can live in our heads; we can avoid loving in general or loving anyone in particular; we can avoid all humor, paradox, and freedom. Even God is not free to act outside of our abstract theological conclusions, yet that is exactly what God does every time God forgives and shows mercy, which is not rational at all. (p. 69)

- In what ways do you recognize yourself in Fr. Richard's list of the ego's payoffs? Which one is your "go-to" tendency? How does it limit you?
- Who is the person you believe God is least likely to forgive? Imagine God forgiving them and having mercy on them anyway. What would be your reaction? How do you think God would respond to you?

28. Reflection

The important thing to note is that the Bible is amazingly uninterested in third-person language—about he, she, or it—although it surely reflects patriarchal worldviews. The much stronger preoccupation of the Bible is the discovery of *second-person language for God!* It is concerned about the direct encounter between two "faces"—God and you, God and the community. What we are aiming for, as this whole chapter asserts, is the possibility of an I-Thou capacity….

I really don't think that the God revealed to us in the Bible cares *what* word we use—as long as it is honest, trustful, and somehow an endearment. (pp. 70-71)

- What is your response to reading the first paragraph above? How have your language choices impacted your understanding of and interaction with God, other humans, and the more-than-human world?

- How would you describe your relationship with God? What words do you use to speak to or with God?

- After reading this chapter of *Things Hidden*, what changes might you want to make in how you approach or interact with God?

CHAPTER FOUR

The Boxing Ring

1. Contemplative Sit

Leading in with the quotation below, practice a contemplative sit. You may wish to set a timer or digital prayer bell for ten, fifteen, or twenty minutes, so that you know when to finish.

- Seat yourself in a quiet area.
- Ground yourself and allow your breathing to settle.
- Notice any tightness in your shoulders and neck and allow any tension in your muscles to relax.
- Allow your back to rest in an aligned, neutral position.
- Once you are settled, read the following passage aloud— this is the opening text for your sit:

This chapter is going to lead you even deeper into what is not a swamp at all, but will feel like it if you are not familiar with biblical themes and directions. But don't be afraid. I am not a heretic, nor is the Bible leading you astray. (p. 73)

- Continue your sit in silence—focusing on your breath, connecting with your body, or by practicing any other method with which you are familiar.
- Allow thoughts, feelings, and sensations to arise, exist, and then fall away while you keep your attention open and large, connecting to that much deeper consciousness.

- Remember, there is no goal. There is no right or wrong way—simply *be* present to what *is* in the moment.

Once finished, you may wish to journal your reflections on this experience.

2. Reflection

Faith will always be faith, and we are never going to be able to make it into total certitude and clarity, although that is always the temptation of religion. (p. 73)

- When in your life have you equated faith with certitude and clarity? Write about that experience in your journal. In what situations are you still inclined to believe this way?
- When have you experienced your faith community equating faith with certitude and clarity? Write about that experience in your journal. How did that experience impact your faith journey, and your relationship with that community?

3. Reflection

The relationship between grace and law ends up being a central issue for almost anyone involved in religion at any depth. Basically, it is the creative tension between religion as requirements and religion as transformation. (p. 74)

- In what ways do you live as if religion is about laws and requirements? How has this informed your understanding and experience of God?
- What would it mean to you to live as if religion is about transformation? What would need to change in your life for you to live this way?

- Describe this "creative tension" Fr. Richard mentions. What makes it creative? Where in your own life do you feel the tension between requirements and transformation?

4. Reflection

Clearly, the easiest way to start, and the way that most people in history have, in fact, started, is with tradition, custom, law, and order: "This is the way we do it." We see that taught very clearly early in the Bible—and it would be the best way to start. (p. 75)

- How were "tradition, custom, law, and order" proclaimed by adults and mentors during your childhood? When and how did people around you deny or contravene such values? What did your earliest experiences teach you about "tradition, custom, law, and order"?
- When have you taught these values to others? How did you feel about the traditions you were passing on? How do you feel about them in light of what you have read in *Things Hidden*?

5. Reflection

There's something about an absolute that compels us, that pulls us into the boxing ring. Absolutes state, "There's something crucial at stake here." In fact, it's our soul. We cannot throw out the very concepts of ideals, absolutes, laws, boundaries, and goals, or we will get nowhere. (p. 75)

- What are the absolutes in your life? Make a list of them and write down why they are absolutes for you. What personal stories and experiences illustrate these absolutes?

- When have you disobeyed, redefined, or "downgraded" an absolute? How do you feel about what you did? At this point, do you believe it was the right choice?

6. Reflection

You must know and respect the rules before you can break the rules.

Now, if you think that is rebellious talk, it probably means you have not studied much of the second section of the Hebrew Scriptures—the Prophets—or the birth of criticism. (p. 76)

- How do you feel about Fr. Richard's statement about knowing and respecting rules before breaking them?
- Think of a time when you broke a rule. Did you know and respect that rule, or were you rebelling without conscious consideration? What is your viewpoint on that experience now? Would you do it again, or not, and why?

7. Reflection

What we do see in the prophetic books is the clear emergence of critical consciousness and interior struggle in Israel....

In a sense, we can call the prophets the fathers and mothers of consciousness, because until we move to self-reflexive, self-critical thinking, we don't move to any deep level of consciousness at all. (p. 76)

- Before you began reading *Things Hidden*, what was your perspective on the Prophets? What has surprised you or changed for you as a result of reading this chapter?
- Define "critical consciousness and interior struggle." Think back over your life and remember a time when such a process was important to you. What happened, and how did that interior struggle help, hinder, and/or change you?

8. Reflection

It is painful but necessary to be critical of your own system, whatever it is. But do know it will never make you popular. As you may know, the prophets are always rejected by their own (see Luke 12:51–52) and usually killed (Luke 13:34). (p. 77)

- When have you been rejected for being "critical of your own system"? Write down what happened, how you felt at the time, and how you feel about it now. Explore whether you would be willing to do the same thing again.

- Would you be willing to claim to be a follower of Jesus, even if that put your life in danger? Who else could suffer if you did? What other considerations would you need to pray about when making such an important decision?

9. *Lectio* Practice

The third section of the Hebrew Scriptures contains the Wisdom books, including, among others, many of the Psalms, Ecclesiastes, the Song of Songs, the Book of Wisdom, and, most especially, the Book of Job. Here we see the clear emergence of what I would like to call non-dualistic thinking. The Hebrew people are finally secure enough to deal with mystery and complex issues that cannot be resolved, that allow no closure, and that demand trust, surrender, and moving to a deeper level that will be called biblical "faith" itself. God, for example, answers none of Job's questions, but rather leads him deeper into mystery. (p. 77)

Slowly read aloud the quotation above four times, following these instructions.

1. With the first reading of the text, allow yourself to *settle in* to the exercise and familiarize yourself with the words. Read the

text out loud, very slowly and clearly. Pause for a breath or two before moving on.

2. For the second reading, *listen* from a centered heart space and notice any word or phrase that stands out to you.

3. After a few moments of silence, read the text a third time, *reflecting* on how this word or phrase is connected to your current life experience. Take a minute to linger over this word or phrase and allow it to engage your body, heart, and awareness of the world around you.

You may want to speak a response aloud or write something in your journal.

4. For the final reading, *respond* with a prayer or expression of what you have experienced, inviting the infinite wisdom of God to support you in places of unknowing, confusion, desire, or hope.

10. Reflection

Remember this: *Transcendence to higher levels of consciousness always means inclusion of the previous levels!* Most reforms and revolutions of history have failed to understand this. This is the genius of the biblical revelation. True wisdom will honor and include both the Law and the Prophets. (p. 78)

- Describe in your own words what it means to "honor and include both the Law and the Prophets" in a life based in wisdom. Include a story (fictional or factual) that illustrates how this would work in your life.
- What feeling words would you use to describe how you view people at other levels of consciousness? What do

these words say about you? What do they say about your own three-steps-forward, two-steps-backward journey toward transcendence?

11. Reflection

The ego is that part of the self that wants to be significant, central, and important. It is very defended and self-protective by its very nature. *It must eliminate the negative to succeed* (Jesus would call it the "actor" in Matthew 23; usually translated from the Greek as "hypocrite"). (p. 78)

- Write down your definition of ego. How is your definition similar and/or different from Fr. Richard's?
- What has been the impact of your ego on your life? What do you tell yourself about your ego?
- What is your response to reading that the Greeks equated ego with "hypocrite"?

12. Reflection

The shadow is that part of the self that we don't want to see, we don't want others to see, and of which we're always afraid. Our tendency is to try to hide it or deny it, even and most especially from ourselves. Jesus, quoting Isaiah, describes it as "listening but not understanding, seeing but not perceiving" (Matthew 13:14–15). Addicts today just call it "denial." (p. 78)

- What has been your experience, if any, of "shadow work"? What has it taught you?
- Remember a time when someone pointed out something about you that you didn't want to believe, but it turned out to be true. How did you respond at the time? What did you learn? What is your perspective on that encounter now?

- What comes to mind when you read the word *denial*? What do you want to deny(!) about it? What might that reveal about you?

13. Reflection

Jesus and the prophets deal with the cause, which is the ego. Our problem is not our shadow self nearly as much as our over-defended ego, which always sees and hates its own faults in other people, and thus avoids its own conversion.

Jesus's phrase for the denied shadow is "the plank in your own eye," which you invariably see as the "splinter in your neighbor's eye" (Matthew 7:4–5). Jesus's advice is absolutely perfect: "Take the plank out of your own eye, and then you will see clearly enough to take the splinter out of your neighbor's eye." (p. 79)

- How is Fr. Richard's interpretation of this passage from Matthew similar and/or different from the way you have read it? Write down what is new for you here, and what it means for you.
- Think about times when you tend to focus on your neighbor's splinter instead of your own plank. What are the feelings behind your tendency? How might you slow down and reframe this tendency and remember to focus on yourself first?
- Spend some time in silence, bringing to mind people you tend to "hate." What "faults" do you hate in them? Ask God to help you see the same "faults" in yourself and work on those instead.

14. Reflection

Jesus is not too interested in moral purity because he knows that any preoccupation with repressing the shadow does not lead us into personal transformation, empathy, compassion, or patience, but invariably into one of two certain paths: denial or disguise, repression or hypocrisy. (p. 80)

- Which is your tendency, denial or disguise? Reflect in your journal about a recent experience of responding with repression or hypocrisy.
- What are you learning about yourself? How would you explain it to others?
- Where do you see the push for "moral purity" in the world around you? How could you respond in a way that's more like Jesus?

15. Reflection

Jesus, instead, is always trying to undercut the arrogance, the self-validation, the cold calculation of the ego. The entire Sermon on the Mount makes that quite clear (Matthew 5–7). He clearly sees *pride, self-sufficiency, and its resultant hypocrisy* as the primary moral problems. (p. 80)

- What do you think Fr. Richard means by self-validation? When have you acted this way, and what happened?
- What does it mean to you to be self-sufficient? How does it feel to have Fr. Richard call it a moral problem?
- Explain why you think Fr. Richard believes self-sufficiency is hypocritical.

16. Reflection

The definition of sin that many of us were given was "a thought, word, or deed contrary to the law of God." The requirements for sin were three: (1) You had to have full knowledge, (2) it had to be a grievous matter, and (3) you had to give it full consent.

That all sounds reasonable at first glance, but actually it's not a definition of biblical sin at all; it's a juridical definition of law. We lost touch with the biblical tradition and the *intimately personal struggle* meant by the word *sin*. We made the whole thing juridical so we could easily identify it, shame it, and enforce it. (p. 81)

- Reread this definition of sin. How does it compare with your understanding of sin?
- Which of your past actions that you've considered "sinful" would match this definition and which would not? What thoughts and feelings arise as you consider this?
- Reflect on your personal experiences of sin and shame. Where does God fit into this process—or not?

17. Reflection

Law is a necessary stage one, but if we stay there, Paul believes—and I often see—it actually becomes a "stumbling stone." It often frustrates the process of transformation by becoming an end in itself. It inoculates us from the real thing. (p. 82)

- What were you taught about laws as a child? In what ways has your perspective on law changed since then, and why?
- Which human laws have you broken and why?
- When has a law interfered with you doing what you felt or believed was the right thing? What was the occasion and what was your response? What did you learn?

18. Reflection

The reason we can move toward real freedom is because we started with moral laws and clear expectations from authority figures, which put good and needed limits to our natural egocentricity. I'll bet most

of you reading this book began rather conservatively. A good therapist
will tell you that predictability, order, and tradition are really the only
way to create a healthy ego structure in the early years. (p. 83)

- Reflect back on your childhood. In what ways did your
experience reflect Fr. Richard's description? In what ways
was your upbringing different?
- Who were the authority figures who most shaped you, and
how did that happen?
- In what ways are you "conservative" today? Why is this
important for you?

19. Reflection

Until people have had some level of inner religious experience, there
is no point in asking them to follow the ethical ideals of Jesus. Indeed,
they will not be able to understand them. (p. 84)

- Take some time in silence to recall your earliest inner
religious experience(s). How did your view of God and/
or Jesus change as a result? What did you see differently
afterward?
- Recall a time when one or more of Jesus's ethical ideals
were confusing to you. What happened to make them
clearer? Which of his teachings are still confusing to
you today?

20. Reflection

What we have done, by and large, is trivialize the law into small issues
that we could obey by willpower, determination, and a certain kind of
reasonableness, while still trying to find salvation through the law.
(Two-thirds of the confessions I heard one day, in my occasional parish
duties, were about missing Mass on Sunday. Only two penitents showed

any significant God-awareness. Most of the confessions were merely laundry lists being brought to the dry cleaner for fear of dirt.) (p. 84)

- What is your experience with the sacrament of confession? In what ways do you see yourself in Fr. Richard's description of confession? In what ways has your experience been different?
- How do you define obedience? What does it mean to you today to be obedient? How has what you are reading influencing your thoughts on obeying the law?

21. Contemplative Sit

Leading in with the quotation below, practice a contemplative sit. You may wish to set a timer or digital prayer bell for ten, fifteen, or twenty minutes, so that you know when to finish.

- Seat yourself in a quiet area.
- Ground yourself and allow your breathing to settle.
- Notice any tightness in your shoulders and neck and allow any tension in your muscles to relax.
- Allow your back to rest in an aligned, neutral position.
- Once you are settled, read the following passage aloud— this is the opening text for your sit:

Morality, which first appears to be the goal and the test of all religion, in time becomes merely the playing field, the theater where the deeper rhythm, the dance of love, shows itself. (p. 84)

- Continue your sit in silence—focusing on your breath, connecting with your body, or by practicing any other method with which you are familiar.

- Allow thoughts, feelings, and sensations to arise, exist, and then fall away while you keep your attention open and large, connecting to that much deeper consciousness.
- Remember, there is no goal. There is no right or wrong way—simply *be* present to what *is* in the moment.

Once finished, you may wish to journal your reflections on this experience.

22. Reflection

We want law for the sake of order, obedience, and "moral purity"; God and Paul want law for the sake of channeling us toward a realization of divine union, to force the honest person to stumble (see Romans 7:7-13; that's really what it says!), and then "fall into the hands of the living God" (Hebrews 10:31). (p. 85)

- Why are laws important for you personally? Why are laws important for you on a communal/social level?
- If you had the chance, would you like to throw out all laws? Why or why not?
- What does it mean to you to "fall into the hands of the living God"? What feelings arise as you imagine doing that?

23. Reflection

Paul tells us in Romans 7:8 that "sin takes advantage of the law" to achieve its own purposes. What does he mean by that? Our unconverted and natural egocentricity ("sin") uses religion for the purposes of gaining self-respect. If you want to hate somebody, want to be vicious or vengeful or cruel or vindictive, I can tell you a way to do it without feeling an ounce of guilt: Do it for religious reasons! Do it thinking you're obeying a law, thinking you're following some commandment or some verse from the Bible. It works quite well. Your untouched egocentricity can and will use religion to feel superior and "right." It is a common pattern. (p. 86)

- When have you hated as Fr. Richard describes here? Remember what you thought and how you felt. Have your thoughts and feelings changed since then, or not?

- When have you been on the receiving end of the hatred Fr. Richard describes here? Remember what you thought and how you felt. How did you respond, and why? Have your thoughts and feelings changed since then, or not?

- How would you define self-respect? How has this definition changed over the course of your life?

24. Reflection

Because we have not taken Jesus's and Paul's teachings seriously, we have often created a religion of smugness—where people who have obeyed the law think they are not sinners. They have "saved" themselves, as it were, and thus think they have little need of mercy, compassion, and the generosity of God. God is a good Enforcer for them, but not the Saving Love revealed to Israel. (pp. 86–87)

- How have you "saved" yourself over the course of your life? What were the results of your efforts?

- Explain your understanding of the difference between God as Enforcer and God as Saving Love.

- In what ways do you live in "a religion of smugness"? How could you change that perspective?

25. Reflection

We have been given a God who not only allows us to make mistakes, but even uses our mistakes in our favor! That is the Gospel economy of grace and is the only thing worthy of being called "good news, and a joy for all the people" (Luke 2:10). If we could have come to God by obedience to laws, there would have been no need for God's love revelation in Jesus. The techniques for order and obedience were already in place. (p. 87)

- When and how did you first learn about the "economy of grace"? What was your response? What is your response to this idea today?
- When have you experienced God using your mistakes in your favor? What happened and how did it affect your faith and your life?
- How would you describe "God's love revelation in Jesus" in your own words?

26. *Lectio* Practice

When you have come out of the boxing ring, the necessary but creative tension of law and grace, you will know that you have won the match—but ironically, you will have won it by losing! (p. 88)

Slowly read aloud the quotation above four times, following these instructions.

1. With the first reading of the text, allow yourself to *settle in* to the exercise and familiarize yourself with the words. Read the text out loud, very slowly and clearly. Pause for a breath or two before moving on.

2. For the second reading, *listen* from a centered heart space and notice any word or phrase that stands out to you.

3. After a few moments of silence, read the text a third time, *reflecting* on how this word or phrase is connected to your current

life experience. Take a minute to linger over this word or phrase and allow it to engage your body, heart, and awareness of the world around you.

You may want to speak a response aloud or write something in your journal.

4. For the final reading, *respond* with a prayer or expression of what you have experienced, inviting the infinite wisdom of God to support you in places of unknowing, confusion, desire, or hope.

CHAPTER FIVE

Good Power and Bad Power

1. Contemplative Sit

Leading in with the quotation below, practice a contemplative sit. You may wish to set a timer or digital prayer bell for ten, fifteen, or twenty minutes, so that you know when to finish.

- Seat yourself in a quiet area.

- Ground yourself and allow your breathing to settle.

- Notice any tightness in your shoulders and neck and allow any tension in your muscles to relax.

- Allow your back to rest in an aligned, neutral position.

- Once you are settled, read the following passage aloud— this is the opening text for your sit:

Only very gradually does human consciousness come to a selfless use of power, or the sharing of power, or even a benevolent use of power—in church, politics, or even family and marriage. Any critique of power is so counterintuitive that we have largely avoided it for most of Christian history. (p. 89)

- Continue your sit in silence—focusing on your breath, connecting with your body, or by practicing any other method with which you are familiar.

- Allow thoughts, feelings, and sensations to arise, exist, and then fall away while you keep your attention open and large, connecting to that much deeper consciousness.
- Remember, there is no goal. There is no right or wrong way—simply *be* present to what *is* in the moment.

Once finished, you may wish to journal your reflections on this experience.

2. Reflection

Watch the news any day, work on a committee, observe a marriage, and you will see that this issue of power has not been well-addressed for most people. (p. 89)

- What is your definition of power? How has it changed over the course of your life?
- What is your experience of power? In what ways have you used it and benefitted from it?
- When and how have others taken advantage of you or abused you with their power? What have you learned from such situations?

3. Reflection

Good power is what Ken Wilber calls "growth hierarchies," which are needed to protect children, the poor, the entire animal world, and all those without power. Bad power is power that is used merely to protect, maintain, and promote oneself. Wilber would call those "dominator hierarchies." He insists, and I agree, that hierarchy is not inherently bad, nor is power. They are just very dangerous for yourself and others if you have not done your spiritual work. (p. 90)

- List some good uses of power, then some bad uses of power. What themes do you notice in your lists?

- In what types of hierarchies are you involved? What is your place in each of those hierarchies? How does your placement influence your perspective and your power?
- Would you agree that protecting yourself is a "bad power"? Why or why not?

4. Reflection

In many liberal circles today, the very notion of hierarchy is rejected, consciously or unconsciously. In contrast, in many conservative circles, dominator hierarchies are often presumed to be the very voice of God. No wonder we so overreact to one another from two such unstable positions. (p. 90)

- Which of Fr. Richard's descriptions of hierarchy better describes your understanding, and why?
- What is your response to Fr. Richard labeling both perspectives as "unstable"?

5. Reflection

This might be the most difficult of all the battles that God seems to have with humanity, although for Christians it should have been resolved in the shared power of the Trinity itself. Here is the dilemma the text creates and does not really resolve: Do a violent people want, create, and need a violent God, or has the textual presentation of a sometimes-violent God legitimated and even blessed our own violent history? Which comes first? (p. 91)

- What do you think of the idea of the "shared power of the Trinity"? How does such a perspective reinforce or change your understanding of God, Jesus, and the Holy Spirit?
- Respond to Fr. Richard's closing question, based on your own experience. If you think both are true, use examples from each viewpoint.

6. Reflection

Two thousand years after the revelation of Jesus, many people still seem to prefer a punitive, threatening, and violent God, which then produces the same kind of people and the same kind of history: If God does it, then we can—and should—too! (p. 91)

- In what ways do you "prefer a punitive, threatening, and violent God"? In what ways do you reject such a God?
- When have you been on the receiving end of people acting in "a punitive, threatening, and violent" way and calling it godly? What happened, how did you feel, and how did you respond? How did it impact your understanding of and feelings about God?

7. Reflection

Psychologically and spiritually, there is no such thing as a triumph by force. Domination is domination, not transformation. How we get there determines where we will finally arrive. The dominated one eventually becomes another dominator, or a sad victim, or both; all of these are liabilities to society and to themselves. You would think we would see that clear pattern in history....

   God alone is patient enough to wait for real change, and powerful enough to know it will happen. (pp. 91–92)

- What is your definition of "transformation"? In what ways do you agree or disagree with Fr. Richard that a spiritual "triumph" cannot be forced?
- When others desire to dominate you, is your tendency to fight, flee, or freeze? How is each option a liability for you and for society?
- How would you describe "real change"?

8. Reflection

Untransformed people seem to think that problems can be solved by external force, which is to change things from the top down or from the outside in....

Dominative power, or what we usually know as political power, is the ability to influence events or others through coercion, punishment, threat, money, the power of our role, or any other external force. It's an illusion that one person can actually change another person; all we can do is externally influence or enforce behavior. (p. 92)

- What are the pros and cons of domination as a use of power?
- When have you tried to change another person? What happened? What impact did that experience have on your understanding of yourself and on your relationship with that person?
- When has another person tried to change you? What happened? What impact did that experience have on your understanding of yourself and on your relationship with that person?

9. Reflection

What the Word of God moves us toward are several kinds of spiritual power. That's where things are not just externally changed, but really transformed, and not transformed from the top down, but from the bottom up; not from the outside in, but rather from the inside out. As Jesus puts it, "Clean the inside of the cup and dish, and the outside will take care of itself" (Matthew 23:26). (p. 92)

- When in your life have you experienced real transformation? What happened? Was there any power at work that you could sense?

- What would be involved in cleaning the inside of your personal cup and dish? What unhelpful perspectives on domination and power do you need to wash away?

10. Contemplative Sit

Leading in with the quotation below, practice a contemplative sit. You may wish to set a timer or digital prayer bell for ten, fifteen, or twenty minutes, so that you know when to finish.

- Seat yourself in a quiet area.
- Ground yourself and allow your breathing to settle.
- Notice any tightness in your shoulders and neck and allow any tension in your muscles to relax.
- Allow your back to rest in an aligned, neutral position.
- Once you are settled, read the following passage aloud— this is the opening text for your sit:

Spiritual power, however, is the ability to influence events and others through our very *being*. Evolved people change others interiorly through *who they are*, and through their sharing of wisdom, rather than through mere external pressure. It *is* a slower process, but much more long-lasting. (p. 93)

- Continue your sit in silence—focusing on your breath, connecting with your body, or by practicing any other method with which you are familiar.
- Allow thoughts, feelings, and sensations to arise, exist, and then fall away while you keep your attention open and large, connecting to that much deeper consciousness.
- Remember, there is no goal. There is no right or wrong way—simply *be* present to what *is* in the moment.

Once finished, you may wish to journal your reflections on this experience.

11. Reflection

The more we try to rely upon external threats, the less we are in touch with our own internal power. They tend to cancel one another out. Conversely, the more we are in touch with our own inner power, the less need we have for any external force, threat, or pressure. (p. 93)

- In what ways do you rely on external threats? What are the results? How do you feel when you employ them?
- In what ways are you in touch with your inner power? How do you utilize it? How do you feel when you do so?

12. Reflection and Activity

We will not trust spiritual power until we have experienced a God who operates in the same way, a God who is willing to wait, allow, forgive, trust, and love unconditionally. It is largely a waste of time to tell people to love generously when the God they have been presented with is a taskmaster who loves quite conditionally, is easily offended and very needy, and threatens people with eternal torture if they do not "believe." (pp. 93–94)

- Mindfully re-read the paragraph above. Which type of God most influenced your childhood? How did that understanding of God influence your life and your faith?
- What has changed in your concept of God during your adulthood? What impact did that have on your faith and in other areas of your life?
- Write a compassionate letter to someone who holds the image of God as taskmaster. What would be important to say to them?

- Write a supportive letter to someone who holds the image of God as trustworthy. What would be important to say to them?

13. Reflection

God is able to use unlikely figures; in one way or another, they are always unable, inept, unprepared, and incapable. The biblical text often shows them to be "powerless" in various ways: Sarah and Abraham; Moses, Rachel, and Rebecca; David, Jeremiah, Job, and Jesus himself are several clear examples. (p. 94)

- With which biblical character do you most readily identify and why? Imagine having a conversation with that person. What do you say? How do they respond?
- When have you seen God use unlikely people—yourself or someone else? Think over what happened and how you sensed God working. What is your response? What is your prayer?

14. *Lectio* Practice

The bottom, the edge, and the outsider are the privileged spiritual positions. That is why the biblical revelation is revolutionary, and even subversive. It is clearly disestablishment literature, yet has largely been used by establishments, which is at the heart of our interpretative problem. (p. 94)

Slowly read aloud the quotation above four times, following these instructions.

1. With the first reading of the text, allow yourself to *settle in* to the exercise and familiarize yourself with the words. Read the

text out loud, very slowly and clearly. Pause for a breath or two before moving on.

2. For the second reading, *listen* from a centered heart space and notice any word or phrase that stands out to you.

3. After a few moments of silence, read the text a third time, *reflecting* on how this word or phrase is connected to your current life experience. Take a minute to linger over this word or phrase and allow it to engage your body, heart, and awareness of the world around you.

You may want to speak a response aloud or write something in your journal.

4. For the final reading, *respond* with a prayer or expression of what you have experienced, inviting the infinite wisdom of God to support you in places of unknowing, confusion, desire, or hope.

15. Reflection

Stop trying. Stop forcing reality. Learn the mystery of surrender and trust, and then it will be done unto you, through you, with you, in you, and, very often, in spite of you. You could say that God's only-and-forever pattern is *creatio ex nihilo*; Yahweh is always "creating something out of nothing." Christian words for the same eternal pattern are "resurrection" or "grace." (p. 95)

- Write down your definition of "grace." Ponder how it relates to Fr. Richard's use of the word here. What do you notice?
- When have you recently kept trying and forcing reality? What was the result? How did you feel about what happened afterward?

- When have you recently been able to surrender and trust? What was the result? How did you feel about what happened afterward?

16. Reflection

The great spiritual and political turnaround is beginning! *The theme of themes (grace, free election, bias toward the bottom) is taking shape.* God is turning the world's values upside down (Acts 17:6). This is where Jesus learned one of his most common and subversive one-liners, "the last will be first and the first will be last." (p. 96)

- How would you explain "bias toward the bottom" to someone who is unfamiliar with the term? What modern example would you use?
- If "God is turning the world's values upside down" today, what would that look like in your life, in your neighborhood, and in your nation?
- When have you seen the last become first? Where would you like to see it happen today and why?

17. Reflection

It seems that until we are excluded from any system, we are not able to recognize the idolatries, lies, or shadow side of that system. It is the privileged "knowledge of the victim." It opens up the playing field, granting equal access to all, if they want it, because *it is no longer a winner's script, which the ego prefers to make it, but actually a life script that now includes these so-called losers.* (p. 97)

- When has someone surprised you by pointing out "the idolatries, lies, or shadow side" of a system? What was your response at that time? How has that change in perspective impacted your life, or not?

- When have you been the one to point out "the idolatries, lies, or shadow side" of a system to others? How did they respond? How did that interaction impact you, or not?
- Do you think of yourself as being one of the "winners" or one of the "losers" as Fr. Richard describes them here? What are your reasons? Can you imagine yourself in the other group?

18. Reflection

Franciscan scholar Ilia Delio...recognizes that *before encounter, God is perceived as omnipotent power. After encounter, God is perceived as humble love.* This has always been the Franciscan emphasis: *God, against all expectation, is humble!* After Jesus, God can no longer be perceived as the Pantocrator or Omnipotence Itself, but as a member of a self-emptying and humble Trinity. Such is the God that Francis discovered in Jesus. (pp. 98–99)

- What was your initial response to Fr. Richard's statement that God is humble? Spend some time in prayer around this idea and notice if/whether/how your initial response changes. Reflect on this in your journal.
- When have you perceived God as omnipotent power? When have you perceived God as humble love? What were the differences in those encounters and your ideas about them?
- Describe your understanding of "the God that Francis discovered in Jesus."

19. Contemplative Sit

Leading in with the quotation below, practice a contemplative sit. You may wish to set a timer or digital prayer bell for ten, fifteen, or twenty minutes, so that you know when to finish.

- Seat yourself in a quiet area.
- Ground yourself and allow your breathing to settle.
- Notice any tightness in your shoulders and neck and allow any tension in your muscles to relax.
- Allow your back to rest in an aligned, neutral position.
- Once you are settled, read the following passage aloud— this is the opening text for your sit:

The human ego hates to change probably more than it hates anything else, and therefore always resists any call to vulnerability or what feels like loss of control. (p. 99)

- Continue your sit in silence—focusing on your breath, connecting with your body, or by practicing any other method with which you are familiar.
- Allow thoughts, feelings, and sensations to arise, exist, and then fall away while you keep your attention open and large, connecting to that much deeper consciousness.
- Remember, there is no goal. There is no right or wrong way—simply *be* present to what *is* in the moment.

Once finished, you may wish to journal your reflections on this experience.

20. Reflection

God has to teach the people that there are alternatives to brute strength. If all we are taught is the art of the hammer, everything in our life is perceived as another nail. Eventually, this broader wisdom becomes the virtues of community, patience, forgiveness, and "cleverness" (see Luke 16:8 and the preceding parable of the crafty steward). (p. 99)

- When and how did you learn there were "alternatives to brute strength"? Do your best to think back to how this understanding changed your life—or not. Reflect on how society would change if this were the accepted perspective.

- Read Luke 16:1–13. How has your reading of *Things Hidden* impacted your understanding of this parable?

- Where can you manifest "the virtues of community, patience, forgiveness, and 'cleverness'" in your own life?

21. Reflection

It might be that God cannot risk giving power to anybody except people who have seen through its illusions and placed their identity elsewhere. All others will misuse power and usually misuse religion too. Thus, even Jesus's three temptations before he begins his public ministry are all temptations to the misuse of power (Matthew 4:1–11). (p. 100)

- Read Matthew 4:1–11. Which temptation to misuse power would be most difficult for you to resist and why?

- When have you seen power misused in religious circles? How did that impact your experience of religion and of faith?

- When have you seen someone using power in ways that felt life-giving? How could you tell it wasn't a misuse of power?

22. *Lectio* Practice

It is the utterly false self that we bring forward for conversion. Merely joining a new group or having an emotional God experience does not usually convert that self at a very deep level, if at all. That is the work of a lifetime of grace, surrender, and prayer. (p. 100)

Slowly read aloud the quotation above four times, following these instructions.

1. With the first reading of the text, allow yourself to *settle in* to the exercise and familiarize yourself with the words. Read the text out loud, very slowly and clearly. Pause for a breath or two before moving on.

2. For the second reading, *listen* from a centered heart space and notice any word or phrase that stands out to you.

3. After a few moments of silence, read the text a third time, *reflecting* on how this word or phrase is connected to your current life experience. Take a minute to linger over this word or phrase and allow it to engage your body, heart, and awareness of the world around you.

You may want to speak a response aloud or write something in your journal.

4. For the final reading, *respond* with a prayer or expression of what you have experienced, inviting the infinite wisdom of God to support you in places of unknowing, confusion, desire, or hope.

23. Reflection

Almost one-third of the psalms are psalms of lament; yet, I am told, these are the least used by the liturgical churches. They both reveal and pave a path for something other than a "winner's script." They allow us to feel, express, and publicly own the downside of things. They allow us to complain to God, and trust that God can receive such complaints. The psalms of lament recognize that we cannot heal what we do not acknowledge. (p. 101)

- What does the word *lament* mean to you? When in your life have you used that term, or heard others use it?

- When have you complained to God? How did you do that, and what happened? Did the process change anything in your outlook, feelings, and/or understanding?
- How could you incorporate lament into your spiritual practice on occasion in some way? What do you imagine the benefits could be?

24. Reflection

Power cannot be inherently bad because it is used by Luke and Paul as a name for the Holy Spirit, who is described as *dynamis*, the ancient Greek word for power...."You will receive power when the Holy Spirit comes upon you. Then you will be my witnesses...to the very ends of the earth" (Acts 1:8). (p. 102)

- What feelings arise in you when Fr. Richard states that power is a name for the Holy Spirit? What impact does this have on your understanding of the Holy Spirit?
- Would you trust yourself with the power described here? Why or why not?

25. Reflection

To span the infinite gap between the Divine and the human, God's agenda is to plant a little bit of God—the Holy Spirit—right inside of us (Jeremiah 31:31–34; John 14:16–26). This is the very meaning of the "new" covenant, and the replacing of our "heart of stone with a heart of flesh" that Ezekiel promised (36:25–26). Isn't that wonderful?

I would say that the Divine Indwelling is *the nexus that differentiates authentic Christian spirituality from all others.* (p. 103)

- What was your first response to reading that "God's agenda is to plant a little bit of God—the Holy Spirit—

right inside of us"? Do you feel this is "wonderful"? Why or why not?

- What would it mean to believe wholeheartedly in this "Divine Indwelling"?
- What would need to change for you to embrace the "Divine Indwelling" more fully?

26. Reflection

Rather than stating that power is bad, the Bible reveals the paradox of power. If the Holy Spirit is power, then power has to be good, not something that is always the result of ambition or greed. In fact, a truly spiritual woman, a truly whole man, is a very powerful person....If we do not name the good meaning of power, we will invariably be content with the bad, or we will avoid our powerful vocation. (pp. 103–104)

- In what ways are you "a very powerful person"? What do you do with that power?
- In what ways do you "avoid [your] powerful vocation"? What could you do with that power?
- How could you regularly check in with yourself about whether you're using power out of "ambition or greed"?

27. Reflection

God wants adult partners who can handle power and critique themselves (see, for example, Hebrews 5:11–6:1).

Do you know why such adults can handle power? First of all, because they don't need it, and secondly, they know it is not their own. Until we don't *need* external power, we normally cannot handle power. When we have real power, we do not need to flaunt it. When we know we are being used by a Higher Power, we do not take our small power too seriously. (p. 104)

- When have you *needed* "external power"? What did you do with that power?

- How have you flaunted power in the past? What was the result? How did you feel about yourself then, and how do the memories make you feel now?

- How do you feel about the idea of being "used by a Higher Power"? What are the pros and cons of letting yourself be used?

28. Reflection

In the New Testament, the twelve apostles are notorious for learning this message very slowly. Right after Jesus teaches them the way of servant leadership, they start arguing about who is the greatest (Mark 9:30-37), and then repeat their silliness again (10:32-45). You must know that this is meant to be a political cartoon; you're supposed to laugh at it all. He just taught them about the path of descent, and they wonder which one of them is going to be the next archbishop! (pp. 104-105)

- What was your response to Fr. Richard's statement that "you're supposed to laugh at it all"? How does it feel to be told to laugh while reading Scripture?

- How seriously do you take Scripture? What would it be like to re-read the gospel stories with a more light-heartedly open perspective?

- In what ways do you tend to learn "very slowly"? When have others tried to help you learn by getting you to laugh? Were you able to laugh with them, or did you get angry or embarrassed? If you couldn't laugh, what could you do to be more open to humor next time?

29. Reflection

The failing Roman Empire needed an emperor and Jesus was used to fill the gap, making much of his teaching literally incomprehensible and unhearable, even by good people. The relationships of the Trinity were largely lost as the very shape of God: The Father became angry and distant, Jesus became the needed emperor, and, for all practical purposes, the Holy Spirit was forgotten. (p. 106)

- In what ways have you been taught and/or experienced God as an "angry and distant" Father? How has this impacted your spirituality and your religious experience?

- In what ways have you been taught and/or experienced Jesus as an "emperor" or similar authority figure? How has this impacted your spirituality and your religious experience?

- What were you taught about the Holy Spirit and how have you experienced it? How has this impacted your spirituality and your religious experience?

- What would you like to change about any or all of these perspectives going forward?

30. Reflection

It is true that wounded and rejected people have a much greater chance of seeing clearly and having something to say. (They also have a greater chance of being bitter!) But Jesus still sends his followers to that place, because *wisdom emerges from what we do with our pain*. It is a unique and needed perspective, as poets, artists, and seers have always understood. (p. 107)

- What do you do with your pain? How has that changed over the course of your life, and why? What impact have those changes had?

- Remember a time when you have found wisdom in what you did with your pain. Take some time to recall what you felt, experienced, and gleaned from that experience. What wisdom do you still hold today as a result of that time?

- Fr. Richard states that "poets, artists, and seers" understand this perspective. What groups of people have taught you the most about this viewpoint? To what individuals or groups do you look for such wisdom today?

31. Reflection

It's not "Preach a deep message and you will be rejected," as we presume. Rather, it's "Be rejected and you will have a deep message to preach." Note that the prophets are almost by definition outside the establishment and always persecuted. (p. 108)

- What is your response to Fr. Richard's reframing of this idea? How does it impact your attitude toward Scripture and Christian tradition?

- What is the deepest message you have learned from someone society rejected? How has it impacted your perspective, your choices, and/or how you follow Christ?

- Who do you think are the prophets in your community today? How are they outside the establishment? How have they been persecuted? How has this impacted their message?

32. Reflection

Note Jesus's basic training for the apostles. He sends them out, away from the group, often in pairs. "Take nothing for your journey—neither staff nor haversack nor bread nor money. Let none of you take a spare tunic" (Luke 9:3).

It's easy to imagine the apostles balking. Who would want to go on such a journey? He's sending them into a situation of certain failure, rejection, and vulnerability, where they have to rely upon other people and upon God. It teaches the way of humble love and trust, and it forces them to look from the outside in. Truthfully, most of us Westerners spend our whole lives looking from the inside out. (p. 109)

- What would be your response to Jesus's "basic training" as Fr. Richard describes it? Be honest with yourself. Could you do what the disciples did, not knowing how things would turn out?

- When have you been sent into a situation "of certain failure, rejection, and vulnerability"? What happened and what did you learn from the experience? How did it impact your perspective on yourself and others?

- Have you ever been forced by circumstance or invitation to experience life from the outside in? What happened and what did you learn from the experience? How did it impact your perspective on yourself and others?

33. Reflection

This austerity was not a program for the whole of life. Rather, it was an initiation rite, a training course in vulnerability and community. Jesus is telling his apostles, as it were, "You've got to go through this or you will never be capable of empathy, compassion, and identification with the pain of the world that you are called to serve. You will use ministry as a career move instead of a servant position." Some such rite of passage seems necessary to break our foundational narcissism. (pp. 109–110)

- What experience in your life has been most like "an initiation rite, a training course in vulnerability and community"? What happened, and what did you learn about yourself?
- When have you approached some aspect of ministry or service as a "career move instead of a servant position"? What happened, and what did you learn about yourself?
- When have you been able to approach some aspect of ministry or service as a servant? What made that experience different?
- How could you identify more with "the pain of the world that you are called to serve"?

34. Reflection

Someone had written these shocking words in chalk on the sidewalk and, since it was early in the morning, they were still there: *"I watch how foolishly man guards his nothing, thereby keeping me out. Truly God is hated here."*

I suspect this was written by an embittered person, but maybe not; maybe she or he was a modern prophet. (p. 110)

- Write the meaning of the chalked message in your own words.
- Do you think the author of the chalked message is embittered, a prophet, or both? Why?
- If you were to meet with the author of the chalked message, what question would you ask?

35. Reflection

Isn't it ironic that most of the Gospel has probably been preached and taught by people who are very comfortable? That's almost an assurance that these preachers will largely miss the point, that they will not preach the true or full message. Jesus made sure his followers were "pilgrims and strangers" (Hebrews 11:13) to business as usual, so they could be "citizens" of a larger realm (Philippians 3:20). (p. 111)

- What do you think is Jesus's "true or full message"? What are the comfortable people missing?
- In what ways are you comfortable with business as usual?
- In what ways are you a pilgrim or stranger to business as usual?
- How has reading *Things Hidden* impacted your understanding of what Jesus wanted his followers to learn and know?

36. Reflection

Almost everybody seems to need some kind of sinner or heretic against which to compare themselves. Judaism is an archetypal religion, and what they do right and wrong illustrates the same pattern as almost all religions. On some level, we all create meritocracies, worthiness systems, and invariably base them on some kind of purity code—racial, national, sexual, moral, or cultural.

Now perhaps we are beginning to see what a radical reformer of religion Jesus was. (p. 112)

- Make a list of the types of people you've defined as outsiders or unworthy over the course of your life. Make another list with the types of people you've defined as insiders and worthy. Sit with these lists in prayer and see what you notice.
- What purity codes do you currently use? What do you think Jesus would say about them?

- In your own words, describe what made Jesus such a radical reformer.

37. Activity

Here is an interesting exercise. Read through the four Gospels and make a two-column list. In one column, list those people who fought Jesus every step of the way. Almost always, they are the people with access to the inner courts of the temple. In the other column, list those people who consistently responded positively to Jesus and his message. Who are these people? They're almost always in those seven groups above who were declared unworthy and kept outside of the temple. (p. 114)

- Re-read Fr. Richard's description of the seven groups that could not enter the temple (pp. 113–114). How many of the seven groups do you belong to?
- Follow Fr. Richard's instructions in the paragraph above. (If reading through all four Gospels feels too daunting, begin with just the Gospel of Mark.) Sit with these lists in prayer and see what you notice.
- Compare these lists with the lists you wrote in the previous exercise. What do you notice? Where are you in alignment with Jesus and where are you out of alignment?

38. Contemplative Sit

Leading in with the quotation below, practice a contemplative sit. You may wish to set a timer or digital prayer bell for ten, fifteen, or twenty minutes, so that you know when to finish.

- Seat yourself in a quiet area.
- Ground yourself and allow your breathing to settle.
- Notice any tightness in your shoulders and neck and allow any tension in your muscles to relax.

- Allow your back to rest in an aligned, neutral position.
- Once you are settled, read the following passage aloud—this is the opening text for your sit:

Remember, *every viewpoint is a view from a point*. The Bible gives us a new and very free viewpoint from which to read the world. But it will only feel like freedom if we do not have a lot to prove and a lot to protect. (p. 115)

- Continue your sit in silence—focusing on your breath, connecting with your body, or by practicing any other method with which you are familiar.
- Allow thoughts, feelings, and sensations to arise, exist, and then fall away while you keep your attention open and large, connecting to that much deeper consciousness.
- Remember, there is no goal. There is no right or wrong way—simply *be* present to what *is* in the moment.

Once finished, you may wish to journal your reflections on this experience.

CHAPTER SIX

THE RAZOR'S EDGE: KNOWING AND NOT KNOWING

1. Contemplative Sit

Leading in with the quotation below, practice a contemplative sit. You may wish to set a timer or digital prayer bell for ten, fifteen, or twenty minutes, so that you know when to finish.

- Seat yourself in a quiet area.
- Ground yourself and allow your breathing to settle.
- Notice any tightness in your shoulders and neck and allow any tension in your muscles to relax.
- Allow your back to rest in an aligned, neutral position.
- Once you are settled, read the following passage aloud— this is the opening text for your sit:

The Bible illustrates both healthy and unhealthy religion, right in the text itself, and Jesus offers us a rather simple criterion by which to judge one from the other. It is not a head category at all, but a visual and practical one: "Does it bear good fruit or bad fruit?" (Matthew 7:15-20; Luke 6:43-45). Jesus is almost embarrassingly practical. (p. 117)

- Continue your sit in silence—focusing on your breath, connecting with your body, or by practicing any other method with which you are familiar.
- Allow thoughts, feelings, and sensations to arise, exist, and then fall away while you keep your attention open and large, connecting to that much deeper consciousness.

- Remember, there is no goal. There is no right or wrong way—simply *be* present to what *is* in the moment.

Once finished, you may wish to journal your reflections on this experience.

2. Reflection

We see in the Bible that orthodoxy is never defined as something that happens only in the head. (In fact, the word is not even in the Bible!) The entire biblical text would emphasize "right relationship" much more than just intellectually being "right." Some call it *orthopraxy, or "right practice." Jesus consistently declares people to be saved or healed who are in right relationship with him, and he never grills them on their belief or belonging systems.* (p. 118)

- How influential has the idea of orthodoxy been in your faith life? How has it impacted the way you relate to God, Jesus, and other human beings?
- Describe "right relationship" in your own words. What would it mean to your experience of faith if you were to focus on right relationships instead of orthodoxy?
- What beliefs are most important to you and why? What do you think Jesus would have to say about those beliefs?

3. *Lectio* Practice

We are walking a thin line here. I am stating that it is important to have correct, orthodox teaching about God, but don't for a moment presume you know everything, or even most things, about God. On that razor's edge, we will find the balance that the Bible offers. (p. 119)

Slowly read aloud the quotation above four times, following these instructions.

1. With the first reading of the text, allow yourself to *settle in* to the exercise and familiarize yourself with the words. Read the text out loud, very slowly and clearly. Pause for a breath or two before moving on.

2. For the second reading, *listen* from a centered heart space and notice any word or phrase that stands out to you.

3. After a few moments of silence, read the text a third time, *reflecting* on how this word or phrase is connected to your current life experience. Take a minute to linger over this word or phrase and allow it to engage your body, heart, and awareness of the world around you.

You may want to speak a response aloud or write something in your journal.

4. For the final reading, *respond* with a prayer or expression of what you have experienced, inviting the infinite wisdom of God to support you in places of unknowing, confusion, desire, or hope.

4. Activity

It is so hard to write about union, about God, or about eternity with any clear credibility, especially in the absence of eyewitness accounts. It always feels like the author is grabbing for words, and the reader knows they are merely approximations. It usually sounds like airy poetry.

The best that spiritual writers can do is to somehow imitate the words of the seraphim to Isaiah: "Holy, Holy, Holy" (Isaiah 6:3), or perhaps today we would say, "Awesome, Awesome, Awesome!" (p. 120)

Sit in silence and recall the most holy moment you have experienced in your life. Remember what happened, what you felt, and what you thought. Reflect on how it has influenced your life. Give thanks to God for that important moment.

You may wish to reflect in your journal following this exercise.

5. Reflection

German Indologist and linguist Heinrich Zimmer…said, "The best things can't be told; the second best are misunderstood." (p. 119)

The second-best things, according to Zimmer, which "are misunderstood," are those things that merely point to the first-best things. Those are things like philosophy, theology, psychology, art, and poetry, all of which—like sacred Scripture—are so easily misunderstood. (p. 121)

- Reflect on when you've been "so easily misunderstood." What were you pointing toward and what happened? Were you eventually able to get your point across, or not?
- How does it feel to have Fr. Richard write that Scripture is one of those things that's "so easily misunderstood"? In what ways have you experienced this to be true?
- Choose one of the disciplines Fr. Richard lists ("philosophy, theology, psychology, art, and poetry") and reflect on how it has been misunderstood. In what ways do you sense that proponents of those disciplines do or don't believe they "are so easily misunderstood"?

6. Reflection

All our words, beliefs, and rituals are merely "fingers pointing to the moon."

I believe Jesus follows the same risky path, which has resulted in him being interpreted in so many different ways (there are now thirty thousand Christian "denominations" worldwide). Apparently, he was willing to take that risk, or he would have written things down. (Did that ever occur to you?) (p. 121)

- Recall a time when you had a discussion with someone where you interpreted the same event or Scripture in different ways. Were you eventually able to come to some resolution, or not? How did you feel about that process?
- What is your response to Fr. Richard's comment that Jesus could have written things down? What thoughts and feelings arise when you consider this possibility?

7. Reflection

Jesus never said, "You must be right!" or even that it was important to be right. He largely talked about being honest and being humble....

The Bible, *in its entirety*, finds a fine balance between knowing and not-knowing, between using words and having humility about words, even though the ensuing traditions have not often found that same balance. "Churchianity," by its very definition, needs to proclaim with absolutes and certainties. (pp. 121–122)

- How important is it for you to be "right"? In what ways has this changed over the years?
- Complete this sentence: Jesus says, "You must be...." Reflect on what your response says about your faith and your understanding of Jesus.
- When have you experienced "Churchianity" proclaiming "with absolutes and certainties"? When have you experienced faithful people "having humility about words"? How would you describe the differences between those two experiences? What did each experience teach you?

8. Reflection

Without an in-depth prayer tradition, religion has cried wolf too many times in history and later been proven wrong. Observe earlier authoritative church statements on democracy, war, torture, slavery, women, usury, anti-Semitism, revolution, liturgical forms, native peoples, the Latin language, and the earth-centered universe—to name a few big ones. If we had balanced our knowing with some honest not-knowing, we would never have made such egregious mistakes. We proved whatever we wanted from one twisted line of Scripture. The unprayerful heart will always twist reality to its own liking. (pp. 122-123)

- Which "earlier authoritative church statements" have impacted you and/or your family of origin? How did they shape your understanding of God and of faithfulness?
- When have you witnessed the balancing of "our knowing with some honest not-knowing"? How did that shape your understanding of God and of faithfulness?
- When have you twisted Scripture to prove what you wanted? How did your twisting impact others? Were the results to your liking in the long term?

9. Reflection

For several centuries, religion in the West has been in a defensive mode—a "siege mentality"—where we needed certainty and clarity and there was little room for not-knowing or the mystical tradition. We are still often in that regressive position today, but now in defense against secularism, New Age thinking, and interfaith dialogue, which all appear, in different ways, to challenge our very sense of identity. (pp. 123-124)

- When have you experienced this "defensive mode" that Fr. Richard describes? What was its impact on you? What was its impact on people who are not like you?

- When have you been tempted to defend Christianity in the way Fr. Richard describes? What has been the result? How have you felt afterward?

- What do you think Jesus would say about "secularism, New Age thinking, and interfaith dialogue"?

10. Reflection

Remember that, unlike the other acts of creation in Genesis, when God divided light from darkness, God did *not* call it "good"! At the very beginning of the Bible, we are warned that we cannot totally separate light from darkness, or the two have no meaning. Genesis brilliantly names *the partial goodness* inside which the whole of creation exists (1:4–5). Remember, *Lucifer* means "Light Bearer," so to think of ourselves as pure light is always demonic.

All things on this earth are a mixture of darkness and light. (p. 124)

- How have you viewed "darkness" over the course of your life? How has that viewpoint changed, and why?

- How have you viewed "light" over the course of your life? How has that viewpoint changed, and why?

- What is your response to Fr. Richard's statement that God did not call the division of darkness and light "good"? What has been your experience of such divisions?

11. Reflection

Jesus is much more of a "lunar" teacher, patient with darkness and growth. He clearly says, "The seed is sprouting and growing, but we do not know how" (Mark 4:27). Jesus seems to be willing to live with such not-knowing, surely reflecting the cosmic patience and certain control of God. When we finally know we are not in charge, we do not have to nail everything down along the way. (p. 125)

- In what areas of your life do you want and try "to nail everything down"? How has that worked for you—or not?
- When have you been invited or forced to live with not-knowing? What was the result? What did you learn?
- How can you become more "patient with darkness and growth"?

12. *Lectio* Practice

Good poetry doesn't try to define an experience as much as it tries to give us the experience itself, just as good liturgy should do. It seeks to awaken our own seeing, hearing, and knowing. It does not give us the conclusion as much as teach us a process whereby we can know for ourselves. (p. 125)

Slowly read aloud the quotation above four times, following these instructions.

1. With the first reading of the text, allow yourself to *settle in* to the exercise and familiarize yourself with the words. Read the text out loud, very slowly and clearly. Pause for a breath or two before moving on.

2. For the second reading, *listen* from a centered heart space and notice any word or phrase that stands out to you.

3. After a few moments of silence, read the text a third time, *reflecting* on how this word or phrase is connected to your current life experience. Take a minute to linger over this word or phrase

and allow it to engage your body, heart, and awareness of the world around you.

You may want to speak a response aloud or write something in your journal.

4. For the final reading, *respond* with a prayer or expression of what you have experienced, inviting the infinite wisdom of God to support you in places of unknowing, confusion, desire, or hope.

13. Reflection

For a spirituality of darkness, the biblical metaphors would be the cave, the Exodus itself, the exile, the belly of the fish, wilderness, and especially desert. A spirituality of light would be represented by mountaintop images, especially Sinai, Horeb, Tabor, and even the Mount of the Beatitudes. (p. 126)

- Which of these biblical metaphors for darkness speaks most powerfully to you and why?
- What metaphor(s) for darkness would you name from your own experience? Reflect on what those metaphors have taught you about faithfulness and the spiritual life.
- Which of these biblical metaphors for light speaks most powerfully to you and why?
- What metaphor(s) for light would you name from your own experience? Reflect on what those metaphors have taught you about faithfulness and the spiritual life.

14. Reflection

The tradition of the mountain is about presence; the tradition of the desert is about absence. The tradition of the mountain is about speaking; the tradition of the desert is about silence. The mountain is about knowing; the desert is about not-knowing. "The pillar of flame by night and the pillar of cloud by day" (Exodus 13:21-22) are both good guides, but we are lost half the time without both! (pp. 126-127)

- Which appeals to you more—desert or mountaintop—and why?
- What could you learn from exploring and embracing the other tradition more fully?
- When has knowing been a trial or a burden?
- When have you benefitted from not-knowing?

15. Reflection

Honeymoon experiences cannot be sustained. We must always leave them and return to the ordinary. What then does Jesus further tell them? "Don't talk about it!" (Matthew 17:9). In Luke's version, at least, it says that they followed his directions (9:36). It was one of the "best things." Jesus knew any talking about it too soon would only weaken the experience. (pp. 127-128)

- Recall a spiritual "honeymoon experience" in your life. Did you try to sustain it? What was the result? Did you try to talk about it? What was the result?
- Explain in your own words why we "must always leave them and return to the ordinary." What is the importance of leaving mountaintop experiences?
- Recall a "best things" experience or idea that you haven't shared with any other human being. What makes it so important or sacred? How has it impacted your life? What about it still falls into the category of not-knowing?

16. Reflection

The fundamentalist mind is a mind that likes answers and explanations so much that it remains willfully ignorant about how history arrived at those explanations, or how self-serving they usually are. Satisfying untruth is more pleasing to us than unsatisfying truth, and full truth is invariably unsatisfying—at least to the small self.

Great spirituality, on the other hand, is always seeking a very subtle but creative balance between opposites....When we go to one side or the other too much, we find ourselves either overly righteous or overly skeptical and cynical. (p. 129)

- What role do answers and explanations play in your life? Are they the bottom line or invitations to further exploration, and why?
- What truths have been unsatisfying for you, and why? What have you done with that dissatisfaction?
- Do you tend toward being "overly righteous or overly skeptical and cynical"? How has this benefitted you? What have you lost or missed when you skewed too much in that direction?
- Where have you witnessed "a very subtle but creative balance between opposites" in the spiritual life? What difference did that make in how you lived out your faith?

17. Contemplative Sit

Leading in with the quotation below, practice a contemplative sit. You may wish to set a timer or digital prayer bell for ten, fifteen, or twenty minutes, so that you know when to finish.

- Seat yourself in a quiet area.
- Ground yourself and allow your breathing to settle.
- Notice any tightness in your shoulders and neck and allow any tension in your muscles to relax.
- Allow your back to rest in an aligned, neutral position.
- Once you are settled, read the following passage aloud— this is the opening text for your sit:

We address human confusion not by falsely pretending to settle all the dust, but by teaching people an *honest and humble process for learning and listening for themselves.* (p. 129)

- Continue your sit in silence—focusing on your breath, connecting with your body, or by practicing any other method with which you are familiar.

- Allow thoughts, feelings, and sensations to arise, exist, and then fall away while you keep your attention open and large, connecting to that much deeper consciousness.

- Remember, there is no goal. There is no right or wrong way—simply *be* present to what *is* in the moment.

Once finished, you may wish to journal your reflections on this experience.

18. Reflection

The Judeo-Christian tradition was not supposed to be a top-down affair, but *an organic meeting between an Inner Knower, accessed by prayer, and the Outer Knower, which we could call Scripture and Tradition.* So much of our fighting over and about Scripture and Tradition is because we have not taught a parallel and equally serious process of prayer. (p. 130)

- In what ways have you experienced the Judeo-Christian tradition as "a top-down affair"? How has that affected your understanding of Jesus? How has it impacted your experience of and with your faith community?

- How do you imagine that "Inner Knower" Fr. Richard references?

- In what ways have you experienced inner knowing and what influence did that have on your life?

19. Reflection

The two paths of knowing and not-knowing are primarily taught through prayer itself. It's no wonder all spiritual teachers emphasize prayer so much.

In Jesus's teaching, we have the prayer of words (what we normally think of as prayer), like saying the Our Father and his encouragement to "ask" (Matthew 7:7–11). From this and the Last Supper, we have developed various forms of social, public, and liturgical prayer, often centering around intercession, gratitude, and worship. (p. 130)

- What "prayer of words" is most important to you and why? What is the history of that prayer?
- Which of the three types of prayer Fr. Richard mentions ("intercession, gratitude, and worship") do you use most often? What would it be like to shift your prayers toward a balance of all three?
- Do you mostly pray in public or in private? What would be the benefits of praying more in a form or way that's different from what you currently do?

20. Reflection

We also have the much-less-taught prayer beyond words: praying "in secret" (Matthew 6:5–6), not "babbling on as the pagans do" (Matthew 6:7), or the predawn, lonely prayer of Jesus (Mark 1:35). These are all pointers toward what many of us today call contemplation. (p. 131)

- What is your experience with contemplation? What does it provide or support that the prayer of words cannot?
- What is your experience with "predawn, lonely prayer"? What are the benefits and drawbacks of praying outdoors, away from others?

- Read Matthew 6:5–8. In your own words, explain why Jesus wanted his disciples to pray "in secret."

21. *Lectio* Practice

Until we have gone through the mystery of transformation from the false self to the True Self, we are not to talk about these things, because we will almost always misuse and misinterpret the experience. We will admire Jesus for miracles instead of waiting for *the real meaning of the miracle, which is always inner transformation.* (p. 132)

Slowly read aloud the quotation above four times, following these instructions.

1. With the first reading of the text, allow yourself to *settle in* to the exercise and familiarize yourself with the words. Read the text out loud, very slowly and clearly. Pause for a breath or two before moving on.

2. For the second reading, *listen* from a centered heart space and notice any word or phrase that stands out to you.

3. After a few moments of silence, read the text a third time, *reflecting* on how this word or phrase is connected to your current life experience. Take a minute to linger over this word or phrase and allow it to engage your body, heart, and awareness of the world around you.

You may want to speak a response aloud or write something in your journal.

4. For the final reading, *respond* with a prayer or expression of what you have experienced, inviting the infinite wisdom of God to support you in places of unknowing, confusion, desire, or hope.

22. Reflection

Islam, Judaism, and Christianity took a great risk in putting religious experience into words. So, God took an even greater risk in the Incarnation, and allowed word to become flesh (John 1:14). The price we have paid for a certain idolatry of words is that the monotheistic religions became the least tolerant of the world's religions. Both Hinduism and Buddhism tend to be much more accepting of others than we are. (p. 133)

- In your own words, explain why it was a risk for Islam, Judaism, and Christianity to put religious experience into words.
- In what ways have you idolized words in your faith life?
- Reflect on a time when you have experienced intolerance from Christians and/or the Christian tradition. How might "a certain idolatry of words" have led to that intolerance?

23. Reflection

Each of the three monotheistic religions insist on absolute truth claims *in forms of words*, whereas Jesus's truth claim was his person (John 14:6), his presence (John 6:35–58), and his ability to participate in God's perfect love (John 17:21–22). Much of the violence of human history has been caused by emphasizing perfect agreement on words and forms (which is never going to happen) instead of inviting people into an experience of the Formless Presence. Jesus gives us *his risen presence* as "the way, the truth, and the life." At that level, there is not much to fight about; in fact, fighting becomes uninteresting. (p. 133)

- Slowly read back through the paragraph above. What is your response to Fr. Richard's interpretation of the meaning of Jesus's words about being "the way, the truth, and the life"?

- How are Jesus's person, presence, and participation in God's love different than truth claims?
- When have you tried to find "perfect agreement on words and forms" with another person or group of people? How did that discussion unfold and what was the result? How did you feel about it afterward?

24. Reflection

We cannot *not* interpret the Bible. Our very reading of the Bible is our interpreting it through our culture, through our temperament, through our personality, through living at a certain time in history, or wherever. That is *always* an interpretation. If we refuse informed interpretation, then we are trapped in our own limited cultural interpretation. Truly, we have no choice. We *must* interpret and we *will* interpret. (pp. 133–134)

- What were you first taught about interpreting the Bible? How has your perspective on interpretation changed over the years?
- What is your response to Fr. Richard's declaration that we "must" and "will" interpret what we read? How could this inform your future reading of Scripture?
- What have you read in the Bible that seems most foreign to you and why?
- What aspect of modern society do you think one of Jesus's disciples would find most foreign and why?

25. Reflection

Only a prayerful, contemplative stance (not either/or thinking) can draw forth those deeper meanings. The only other major time we tend to move out of dualistic thinking is during times of darkness, sorrow, and loss. Thus, I think *love and suffering are the two primary paths of transformation.* (p. 134)

- When has "a prayerful, contemplative stance" brought forth new or deeper meaning for you? What was your response?
- When and how has suffering transformed you? In what ways were you aware of God's presence during that time, or afterward, or not at all?
- When and how has love transformed you? In what ways were you aware of God's presence during that time, or afterward, or not at all?

26. Reflection

We must accept the literary forms in which sacred Scripture is written, just as we understand the difference between nonfiction, novels, poetry, and research papers when we go to the library. If not, we end up in today's fundamentalist dead-end: insisting on conclusions that are not there and are often contradicted in other texts (which are then ignored), condemning things Jesus never once talked about (homosexuality and birth control), and legitimating things that Jesus strongly criticized (wealth and violence). I am not taking a stance here on these issues, but I am pointing out our utter inconsistency. (pp. 134–135)

- Where have you noticed Christianity's "utter inconsistency"? How has it impacted your willingness to accept other aspects of the faith?
- What faith stances have you taken in the past that you don't take now? What change(s) in your life or understanding supported this shift?

- What scriptural contradictions still trouble you today? In what ways is reading *Things Hidden* proving helpful and/ or challenging in this regard?

27. Contemplative Sit

Leading in with the quotation below, practice a contemplative sit. You may wish to set a timer or digital prayer bell for ten, fifteen, or twenty minutes, so that you know when to finish.

- Seat yourself in a quiet area.
- Ground yourself and allow your breathing to settle.
- Notice any tightness in your shoulders and neck and allow any tension in your muscles to relax.
- Allow your back to rest in an aligned, neutral position.
- Once you are settled, read the following passage aloud— this is the opening text for your sit:

We must approach the Scriptures with humility and patience, with our own agenda out of the way, and allow the Spirit to stir the deeper meaning for us. Otherwise, we only hear what we already agree with or what we have decided to look for....This mode of teaching is much more about transformation than information. That changes the entire focus and goal. (p. 135)

- Continue your sit in silence—focusing on your breath, connecting with your body, or by practicing any other method with which you are familiar.
- Allow thoughts, feelings, and sensations to arise, exist, and then fall away while you keep your attention open and large, connecting to that much deeper consciousness.
- Remember, there is no goal. There is no right or wrong way—simply *be* present to what *is* in the moment.

Once finished, you may wish to journal your reflections on this experience.

28. Reflection

There are certain truths that can be known only if we are sufficiently emptied, sufficiently ready, sufficiently confused, or sufficiently destabilized. That's the genius of the Bible! It doesn't let us resolve all these questions in theology classrooms. In fact, *none* of the Bible appears to be written out of or for academic settings.

It is very clear that Jesus was able to heal, touch, teach, and transform people, and there was no prerequisite for any formal education.... Jesus, as a teacher, largely talked about *what was real and what was unreal*, and therefore how we should live inside of that reality. It required humility and honesty much more than education. (pp. 135–136)

- How has reading *Things Hidden* made you "sufficiently emptied, sufficiently ready, sufficiently confused, or sufficiently destabilized"?
- What non-classroom experiences have brought you to unexpected truths and what has been the influence of those experiences on your life?
- When in your life have "humility and honesty" opened the door to deeper wisdom?

29. Reflection

It was Jesus's concrete examples that broke people through to the universal light. Particulars seem to most open us up to universals, which is what poets have always understood.

"Thisness" is the actual spiritual doorway to the everywhere and the always, much more than concepts. Storytellers seem to know that better than theologians. (p. 136)

- When has something concrete opened you up to a universal truth or understanding? Describe what happened and its impact on your life.
- Recall the work of a favorite storyteller. Perhaps you may wish to revisit a treasured book or video. Notice how they teach "universals" through particular situations, people, and experiences.
- Bring to mind your favorite of Jesus's parables. What universal(s) is he illustrating? How has that parable influenced your spiritual journey?

30. Reflection

A journey of faith is going to create a people of faith. You cannot give people the conclusions without walking the journey, or they will substitute the conclusions for the journey itself. Maybe that will always be the downside of religion, for that is what it most often does. The container becomes the substitute for the actual contents in the container. (p. 137)

- When has someone tried to give you the conclusion instead of inviting you on the journey? What was your response? If you accepted the lesson without taking the journey, how did that impact your faith life?
- When have you grown in faith by "walking the journey"? What were the benefits of taking that route?
- Describe in your own words the difference between the container and the contents that Fr. Richard describes here. Over the course of your life, have you been more interested in the container or the contents?

31. Reflection

Only people who have first lived and loved, suffered and failed, and lived and loved again, are in a position to read the Scriptures in a humble, needy, inclusive, and finally fruitful way. If you put the Scriptures in the hands of a person uninitiated by life, they will always make it into a head trip. It becomes a set of *prescriptions* instead of an actual *description* of what is real and what is unreal. (p. 138)

- What faith "prescriptions" were you raised with? How well have they held up under the pressure of having "lived and loved, suffered and failed"?
- What life experiences have taught you to be "humble, needy, inclusive"?
- Describe one way that your life experience has influenced your reading of Scripture. Did that experience make you more or less open to further changes, and why?

32. Reflection

Any glib use of the name of God, therefore, is somehow "in vain" and *always* irreverent. To speak God's name is always somehow to trivialize it. This religious humility was taught to the Jewish people at the very beginning. Unfortunately, that same humility did not extend to our entire understanding of spiritual things and to the limits of language in general. We would have done well to take this cosmic caution to the whole world of God talk, but we thought it was about cussing! (p. 139)

- When and how do you tend to "use the name of God"? In what ways do you trivialize it?
- What would have to change if you took the second commandment—"You shall not speak the name of God in vain" (Exodus 20:7)—seriously?
- In what ways has reading this chapter of *Things Hidden* influenced your understanding of "the whole world of God talk"?

33. Activity

Some Jewish scholars say that the consonants used in the spelling of YHWH are the very few that do not allow us to close our mouths around them, or even significantly use our lips or tongue; in fact, *they are very likely a brilliant attempt to replicate human breathing: YH on the captured in breath, and WH on the offered out breath!* (Stop reading and literally take a breath on that one!) (pp. 139–140)

Find a quiet space where you can be alone and set a timer for ten minutes. Then follow Fr. Richard's instructions to breathe the name of YHWH, in and out.

You may wish to reflect in your journal following this exercise.

34. Reflection

God's eternal mystery cannot be captured or controlled, but only received and spoken, as freely as the breath itself—the one single thing we have done since the moment we were born and will one day cease to do in this body. God is as available and accessible as our breath itself, and no religion is going to be able to portion that out, control it, or say who gets it and who doesn't. (p. 140)

- What feelings arise in you as you read the paragraph above? What response is it calling forth in you?
- What would change in your life if you truly believed and lived with God being "as available and accessible as our breath itself"? How could it transform your action and your prayer?

35. Contemplative Sit

Leading in with the quotation below, practice a contemplative sit. You may wish to set a timer or digital prayer bell for fifteen, twenty, or twenty-five minutes, so that you know when to finish.

- Seat yourself in a quiet area.
- Ground yourself and allow your breathing to settle.
- Notice any tightness in your shoulders and neck and allow any tension in your muscles to relax.
- Allow your back to rest in an aligned, neutral position.
- Once you are settled, read the following passage aloud— this is the opening text for your sit:

Let your breathing in and out, for the rest of your life, be your prayer to—and from—such a living and utterly shared God. You will not need to prove it—nor can you—to anybody else. Just keep breathing with full consciousness and without resistance, and you will know what you need to know. (p. 141)

- Continue your sit in silence—focusing on your breath, connecting with your body, or by practicing any other method with which you are familiar.
- Allow thoughts, feelings, and sensations to arise, exist, and then fall away while you keep your attention open and large, connecting to that much deeper consciousness.
- Remember, there is no goal. There is no right or wrong way—simply *be* present to what *is* in the moment.

Once finished, you may wish to journal your reflections on this experience.

CHAPTER SEVEN

Evil's Lie

1. Contemplative Sit

Leading in with the quotation below, practice a contemplative sit. You may wish to set a timer or digital prayer bell for fifteen, twenty, or twenty-five minutes, so that you know when to finish.

- Seat yourself in a quiet area.
- Ground yourself and allow your breathing to settle.
- Notice any tightness in your shoulders and neck and allow any tension in your muscles to relax.
- Allow your back to rest in an aligned, neutral position.
- Once you are settled, read the following passage aloud—this is the opening text for your sit:

The Bible, as I will continue to state, is a "text in travail," struggling toward its conclusions and only getting the point step by step, and frequently stepping backward. The important thing is to stay in the process, stay with the unfolding text and allow it to lead you forward. (p. 143)

- Continue your sit in silence—focusing on your breath, connecting with your body, or by practicing any other method with which you are familiar.
- Allow thoughts, feelings, and sensations to arise, exist, and then fall away while you keep your attention open and large, connecting to that much deeper consciousness.

- Remember, there is no goal. There is no right or wrong way—simply *be* present to what *is* in the moment.

Once finished, you may wish to journal your reflections on this experience.

Before proceeding further, you may wish to review the Staying within Your Comfort Zone section of the Introduction to this Companion Guide.

2. Reflection

The human delusion seems to be this: We think someone else is always the problem, not ourselves. We tend to export our hate and evil elsewhere. In fact, this problem is so central to human nature and human history that its overcoming is at the heart of all spiritual teachings. What mature spirituality tries to do is to always keep our own feet to the fire. (pp. 143-144)

- Recall a recent time when you have thought someone else was "the problem." Can you see echoes of that "problem" in yourself?
- Under what circumstances do you "export" your "hate and evil elsewhere"? Which specific hatreds and evils do you tend to focus on? Have others seen those specific problems in you?
- How could you keep your own "feet to the fire" to recognize when and how a problem is yours rather than someone else's?

3. Reflection

Human nature always wants either to play the victim or to create victims—and both for the purposes of control. In fact, the second follows from the first. Once we start feeling sorry for ourselves, we will soon find someone else to blame, accuse, or attack—and with impunity! It settles the dust quickly, and it takes away any immediate shame, guilt, or anxiety. (p. 144)

- Which role have you most frequently assumed in life: "to play the victim or to create victims"? Do you concur with Fr. Richard's assessment that "the second follows from the first"? Why or why not?
- When have you found "someone else to blame, accuse, or attack"? What were your underlying motives? What was the result? How did you feel about yourself afterward?

4. Reflection

Hating, fearing, or diminishing someone else holds us together, for some reason. The creating of necessary victims is in our hard wiring. René Girard called "the scapegoat mechanism" the central pattern for the creation and maintenance of cultures worldwide since the beginning.

The sequence, without being too clever, goes something like this: We compare, we copy, we compete, we conflict, we conspire, we condemn, and we crucify. (p. 144)

- Recall a time when you witnessed "the scapegoat mechanism" in action. What happened and how were you involved? What did you feel about it during the event and after it was over? What are your thoughts and feelings about that incident today?
- When have you been some person or group's "necessary victim"? What happened? How did you feel about yourself at the time, and how do you feel about that event today?

- Which elements of Fr. Richard's sequence are easiest for you to unconsciously participate in or agree to? How might you respond more consciously in the future?

5. Reflection

It's hard for us religious people to hear, but the most persistent violence in human history has been sacred violence, or, more accurately, *sacralized* violence. Human beings have found a most effective way to legitimate their instinct toward fear and hatred. They imagine that they are fearing and hating on behalf of something holy and noble, like God, religion, truth, morality, their children, or love of country. It takes away our guilt, and we can even think of ourselves as representing the moral high ground, or being responsible and prudent, as a result. (p. 145)

- When have you used God or religion to legitimize your violent thoughts or actions? What was violent about your actions or ideas? How do you view them now, in light of Fr. Richard's words?
- In what circumstances do you take "the moral high ground"? How does it feel to do this? What do those feelings tell you about yourself?

6. Reflection

It never occurs to most people that they can become what they fear and hate. It is a well-kept secret. Without wisdom, it all appears like a wonderful and moral thing, like "protecting my children." (p. 145)

- Have you ever noticed yourself becoming someone you "fear and hate," or even someone you just don't like? Spend some time reflecting on what happened and see if you can find some hidden violence there, toward yourself and/or toward others.

- What violence do you consider justified and why?

7. Activity

Scapegoating or sacralized violence is the best possible disguise for evil. We can concentrate on evil "over there" and avoid our own. Evil is never easily recognized as evil by those who do it. As Paul so wisely writes, "Satan disguises itself as an angel of light" (2 Corinthians 11:14). We all choose *apparent goods* inside our own unrecognized frame of reference. *Your* violence is always bad and evil, while *mine* is always necessary and good. (p. 145)

- Make a list of the evils that you see "over there." Next, make a list of evils that you have witnessed within yourself, your society, and the groups (including church communities) of which you are a part. Then compare the lists. What do you notice?
- Make a list of the "apparent goods" that you see within yourself, your society, and the groups (including church communities) of which you are a part. Next, make a list of the goods that you see "over there." Then compare the lists. What do you notice?
- Reflect in your journal what this exercise has revealed to you about your notions and perspectives on good and evil.

8. Reflection

I've met many holy people around the world, but I've also encountered people that I'd have to describe as evil. If I would try to describe the evil people and evil events that I've encountered, they're invariably characterized by a sense of certainty and clarity. They suffer no self-doubt or self-criticism, smirking at people who would dare to question them. They own no shadow from their side, which is always a sign that their evil has been projected elsewhere. Often, they are overtly religious. Remember, the very term Satan means "the accuser." Be careful when you see yourself accusing or, as Jesus says, "throwing stones" (John 8:7). It is the satanic disguise, a marvelous diversionary tactic. (p. 146)

- How did it feel to read Fr. Richard's description of "evil people and evil events"? Did someone or some event spontaneously spring to mind? In what ways would you confirm and/or add to Fr. Richard's description?

- If this feels like an exercise you can do safely, intentionally recall when you have encountered someone who fits Fr. Richard's "evil people" description. What was the situation, and what was your response to that person at the time?

- When have you witnessed someone using religion in a way that you thought or felt was evil—at the time, or later on? When have you done it yourself? What has Fr. Richard's teaching shown you about such tendencies?

9. Reflection

Like all addictive thinking, scapegoating shows itself as "all or nothing" thinking, totally either/or, with no capacity for paradox and little tolerance for ambiguity. I would describe such people as "split"; Jesus calls them "actors" at least eleven times in Matthew 23:13–29, though it is usually translated as "hypocrites." The English word has come to mean *malicious* people, but probably it more often means *deceived* people. (p. 146)

- Recall an encounter you've had with someone who fits Fr. Richard's description. How does his explanation reframe that encounter? What does it reveal for you about the idea of addictive thinking?

- Honestly assess your own tendency toward "'all or nothing' thinking, totally either/or, with no capacity for paradox and little tolerance for ambiguity." How has this influenced your tendency to judge, condemn, and/or scapegoat others?

- In your own words, describe what you think Fr. Richard means by "probably it more often means *deceived* people."

10. Reflection

"They know not what they do," as Jesus says (Luke 23:34) of those who kill him, which is probably why he thinks of them as actors more than sinners. They are mostly unconscious—living out of the dominant consciousness—more than directly malicious. Most evil is done by unconscious people, in my opinion. If we were aware and awake, we would see right through it all—and never do it! (p. 146)

- In what ways are you "living out of the dominant consciousness"? Explain how this makes you "unconscious" and what impact this has on your choices.

- What's the closest you've been to participation in or witnessing of a violent mob? To the extent you can do this safely, recall your thoughts and feelings at the time. Thinking back on the event, in what ways were mob participants "actors more than sinners"? In what ways do you believe they were actually "sinners"?

- When have you been "aware and awake" enough to know an attitude or action was wrong or evil? What supported that "aware and awake" perspective? How might you nurture that perspective in yourself?

11. Reflection

At some level, persons of faith are invariably unsure of their own understanding and are asking God, "Is this the right thing to do?" or, like Mary, "How can this come about?" (Luke 1:34). The faith stance is humble about its capacity to know the whole picture, as I noted in the last chapter. Evil is always sure of itself, and goodness is not. I believe that to be true.

Goodness, however, is accompanied by peace and patience, and even "consolation," as Saint Ignatius of Loyola (1491–1556) taught his Jesuits. That is more than enough payoff for sustaining some doubt and ambiguity. (p. 147)

- When have you been sure of yourself, only to learn later that your stance was incorrect or unhelpful? What did that experience teach you about yourself?
- How does it feel to have Fr. Richard describe "persons of faith [as] invariably unsure of their own understanding"? What impact does this have on your understanding of faith?
- Describe what it's like for you to not have the "capacity to know the whole picture." What would need to shift for you to be able to embrace the "peace and patience, and even 'consolation'" that Fr. Richard describes?

12. Reflection

The genius of the biblical text is that this capacity for course correction, for self-critique, is actually contained in the book itself. That is necessary and good criticism. In other words, the whole of the Bible unlocks itself from within, by showing us both the capacity to get the point and our endless capacity to miss the point, which it calls *sin* (*hamartia*, "missing the mark"). (pp. 147–148)

- Recall a biblical story in which someone illustrates *hamartia*. In your own words, describe how the Bible demonstrates this "capacity...for self-critique." What has this biblical story taught you about your own need for "course correction"?

- Define the word *criticism* as you have understood it. How has Fr. Richard's use of the phrase "good criticism" changed or expanded your understanding?

- What feelings arise in you in response to Fr. Richard's statement that we have an "endless capacity to miss the point"? Where do you find hope?

13. Reflection

Until now, rather than generating its own criticism from within, Christianity has most often been criticized from the outside, by its enemies, who often do not know Christianity's inner values. When criticism is allowed and encouraged from within, however, that criticism is subject to Judeo-Christian values and criteria. In other words, it needs to be accountable to the Tradition and criticized by its own accepted values. This is what Moses, Jesus, and Paul do from within the text during their lifetimes, and why they are true reformers. (p. 148)

- When have you witnessed Christianity being "criticized from the outside"? In what ways do you feel those criticisms are valid? Do you think those issues could have been addressed with "good criticism" from the inside? What does this reflection have to say to you about the value of criticism?

- When have you witnessed Christianity being held "accountable to the Tradition"? What was the result, and what did you learn from what you witnessed?
- Describe a "true reformer" in your own words.

14. Reflection

In fairness, those outside critics are often looking outside of themselves at someone else's sin. They usually have not benefited from the revelation of the scapegoat mechanism and waste an awful lot of time accusing other people of their faults. That is what I would mean by bad criticism, along with any criticism that is negative in intent, mean-spirited, and does not build up anybody or anything. However, that does not mean we cannot still use negative criticism for our own good and growth, even if it sometimes comes from malicious intent. If it is even partly true, it might be from the Holy Spirit. (p. 149)

- When have you witnessed what Fr. Richard describes as "bad criticism" of the church? What made it "bad"? Did you feel the criticism was justified anyway?
- Recall a time when you received "negative criticism" that was "partly true." What helped you to see beyond the mean-spirited intent to the kernel of truth? How might you bring that inner stance or perspective to future situations?

15. Reflection

God loves, it seems, but at this stage God's love is still exclusive and determined by the worthiness of the receiver. We are not yet ready for a love that is determined by the abundance of the Giver. It is going to take us a long time to get to the point where we realize God's love is self-determined instead of being determined by our behavior. (p. 150)

- In what ways do you believe "God's love is...determined by the worthiness of the receiver"? Reflect on what lies at the root of that viewpoint. What would need to happen for you to believe differently?

- When have you experienced God's abundance? Reflect on how you were able to believe that the abundance came from God. What would happen in your life if you could believe in God's abundance in every situation?

- Explain in your own words how "God's love is self-determined."

16. Reflection

The text reveals and creates a problem for us, and then at least partially unlocks it: "Do you think it was because you were greater than the other nations, that Yahweh set his heart on you? No, you were the least of all the peoples....Yahweh was being true to his own graciousness in loving you" (Deuteronomy 7:7, 9). So, we still have God justifying violence, it seems, but at least Yahweh is telling them that they are not any better than anyone else, and their election is absolutely free from God's side and undeserved from theirs. Yahweh reveals the Godself as "gracious," and now the hope is that this will rub off on them. (p. 151)

- When have you been taught that your nation, church, or other group was "greater than the other"? Do you still believe that about any groups to which you belong? How would you explain that stance in response to Fr. Richard's teaching?

- How does Fr. Richard's teaching here influence your understanding of the God of Hebrew Scripture? Reflect on how your reading of *Things Hidden* is affecting your relationship with God.

- What is your response to Fr. Richard's statement that the Hebrew people's "election is absolutely free from God's side and undeserved from theirs"?

17. Reflection

Remember, what makes us holy can also make us evil. After any real religious encounter, people are normally dangerous for a few weeks or months, because religious experience necessarily makes us think we are the center of the world. God, it seems, has to take that risk every time God chooses us and loves us. We can utterly misuse that ego inflation for self-advancement instead of generative love. *Self-centered people misuse human love, and they will do the same with divine love.* (p. 152)

- Recall a powerful "religious encounter" or experience in your life. How did it impact your attitude toward yourself? In what ways could you have been "dangerous" afterward—and were you? How do you view any shift in self-understanding now?
- When have you felt you were "the center of the world"? Did you misuse that feeling for "self-advancement" in any way? Why or why not?
- Describe a time when you witnessed a self-centered person misusing divine love. What happened, and what did it teach you? In what ways might you need to reframe that understanding in light of Fr. Richard's words?

18. Reflection

We must learn from those texts that move us beyond our natural desire for ego security, status needs, and group idolatry. Only then can we trust that it is God who is breaking into human consciousness—and into the text. But how can we trust that we are following the correct tangent? By noting the trim of the sails. Where is the tack of the text directing us? This is precisely the meaning of the Christian affirmation that Jesus is the fulfillment of the Scriptures. The sails are set for a God of suffering and humble love, as we finally see in Jesus. Only because of him are we totally assured that God is beyond tribalism, violence, hatred, and validating the vanities of the small self. (p. 152)

- What is your favorite Bible verse? Slowly read through the context or entire chapter where that verse occurs and notice "the trim of the sails." In what ways does it reinforce and/or "move us beyond our natural desire for ego security, status needs, and group idolatry"?

- What passage(s) in the Bible would you quote to describe "a God of suffering and humble love"? If nothing comes to mind, re-read one of the gospels and notice where Jesus exemplifies those qualities.

- How would you explain to someone how Jesus "is beyond tribalism, violence, hatred, and validating the vanities of the small self"?

19. Contemplative Sit

Leading in with the quotation below, practice a contemplative sit. You may wish to set a timer or digital prayer bell for fifteen, twenty, or twenty-five minutes, so that you know when to finish.

- Seat yourself in a quiet area.

- Ground yourself and allow your breathing to settle.

- Notice any tightness in your shoulders and neck and allow any tension in your muscles to relax.

- Allow your back to rest in an aligned, neutral position.

- Once you are settled, read the following passage aloud—this is the opening text for your sit:

Jesus does not define holiness as separation from evil as much as the absorption and transformation of it, wherein I pay the price instead of always asking others to pay the price. (p. 153)

- Continue your sit in silence—focusing on your breath, connecting with your body, or by practicing any other method with which you are familiar.
- Allow thoughts, feelings, and sensations to arise, exist, and then fall away while you keep your attention open and large, connecting to that much deeper consciousness.
- Remember, there is no goal. There is no right or wrong way—simply *be* present to what *is* in the moment.

Once finished, you may wish to journal your reflections on this experience.

20. Reflection

Education is not the same as transformation. You'd think that, if we would educate people, they would stop scapegoating. Yet all I see is that scapegoating becomes more sophisticated among intellectuals. (p. 154)

- What was the attitude toward education in your family of origin? What lessons about the value of education have you absorbed from society? How have these impacted your attitude toward education today?
- Describe the differences between education and transformation in your own words. When and how have you seen people or church communities confusing or conflating the two?

- Why do you imagine education is insufficient on its own to spark transformation?

21. Reflection

So, I will pose the great spiritual problem in this way: "How do we stand against hate without becoming hate ourselves?" We would all agree that evil is to be rejected and overcome; the only question is, how? How can we stand against evil without becoming a—denied—mirror image of the same? That is often the heart of the matter which, in my experience, is only resolved successfully by a very small portion of people, even though it is quite clearly resolved in the life, teaching, and death of Jesus. (pp. 154–155)

- Take some time to prayerfully respond to the questions Fr. Richard raises here. What do you see about yourself, your faith, and your understanding of human nature in your responses?
- Using your own words, describe one example where Jesus stood against hate without becoming hate himself.
- What is your felt response to Fr. Richard's statement that only "a very small portion of people" are able to "successfully" resolve these questions? How important is it for you to wrestle with these issues yourself and why?

22. Reflection

Some have called this part of Revelation [5:6–8:1] the "Lamb's War," which is a totally different way of dealing with evil—absorbing it in God (which is the real meaning of the suffering body of Jesus) instead of attacking it outside. It is undoubtedly the most counterintuitive theme of the entire Bible, although much of the bellicose and violent imagery in the rest of the book of Revelation probably undoes any Lamb's War message, at least in that book. The book of Revelation is indeed a text in *great* travail! Immature people will almost always misuse it. (p. 156)

- Thoughtfully read Revelation 5:6—8:1. What do you notice? To what extent do you agree with Fr. Richard's description of "dealing with evil" by "absorbing it in God"? How does this influence your perspective on the book of Revelation? How could this inform your own future encounters with evil?
- When have you experienced "immature people" misusing the book of Revelation? In what ways does Fr. Richard's description shift your understanding of how Revelation is *meant* to be read and used?

23. Reflection

There is at least one further example of our theme in the historical books and that is the marvelous story of Gideon in Judges 6–8. Yahweh keeps cutting down Gideon's army, saying, "There are too many people with you for me to put Midian into your power, or you might claim the credit at my expense. You might say, 'My own hand has rescued me'" (7:2).

Slowly, Yahweh whittles Gideon's troops down from 33,000 to 300! But the direction is clear: The text is ever-so-slowly moving us from a total trust in violence to a trust in nonviolence and spiritual transformation. (p. 157)

- When have you trusted in violence and why? How has this trust evolved over time and who has influenced the evolution?
- When have you trusted in nonviolence and why? How has this trust evolved over time and who has influenced the evolution?

- When are you tempted to say, "My own hand has rescued me"? What internal change would need to happen for you to trust in God instead?

24. Reflection

Universalism (non-groupthink) is the point of the whole book of Jonah. Jonah doesn't want to go and preach to the Ninevites because, like a member of any group, he does not like his God caring about other people. God has to shipwreck him and, through the marvelous imagery of the big fish, spit him up on the very shore from which he is fleeing. Jonah moves into a jealous and resentful rage (4:1, 4, 9) when the Ninevites actually believe his message (3:5). So, Yahweh says to Jonah in the last verse of the book, "Am I not free to feel sorry for Nineveh?" (4:11). The foundation is being laid for a universal compassion, not just a small superiority system, which is what Jonah, the unwilling prophet, seems to want. (p. 158)

- In what ways does Fr. Richard's description of the book of Jonah align with or contradict your understanding of this story? How does his retelling influence your feelings about Jonah?
- What are your feelings about universalism? What is it like to have this story used to reinforce the message? What would need to change for you to embrace this perspective?
- What would it mean for the world that God has compassion for everyone, not just certain groups?

25. *Lectio* Practice

We'll find texts of violence and nonviolence in both Hebrew and Christian Scriptures, but the deepest and utterly new revelation in both Testaments is that God is not violent, in spite of the violence of the people among whom God dwells. As Jesus puts it, "God's sun rises on the good and the bad; God's rain falls on the just and the unjust." (pp. 158–159)

Slowly read aloud the quotation above four times, following these instructions.

1. With the first reading of the text, allow yourself to *settle in* to the exercise and familiarize yourself with the words. Read the text out loud, very slowly and clearly. Pause for a breath or two before moving on.

2. For the second reading, *listen* from a centered heart space and notice any word or phrase that stands out to you.

3. After a few moments of silence, read the text a third time, *reflecting* on how this word or phrase is connected to your current life experience. Take a minute to linger over this word or phrase and allow it to engage your body, heart, and awareness of the world around you.

You may want to speak a response aloud or write something in your journal.

4. For the final reading, *respond* with a prayer or expression of what you have experienced, inviting the infinite wisdom of God to support you in places of unknowing, confusion, desire, or hope.

26. Reflection

Remember, both Peter and Paul still understood Jesus's very adamant teaching on servant leadership (Luke 22:24–27; John 13:14–16, etc.). Our later fascination with dominative power finds no basis in Jesus, but instead set loose a spiral of violence throughout Christian history, as groups and individuals reacted against church authority. We do not need or desire to react against servants, whereas kings usually call forth "an equal and opposite reaction," to borrow Isaac Newton's description of nature. I wonder if we can ever regain the trust that Jesus placed in us. (p. 160)

- What is your perspective on church authority? In what ways has it been used for and/or against you and the groups to which you belong?
- Imagine you were Paul, writing a letter to your church community today. What would you say about their use and/or abuse of authority and dominative power?
- What do you believe it would take to "regain the trust that Jesus placed in us"?

27. Reflection

Jesus's life and his teaching are starkly opposed to that perennial, universal mistake that is probably happening every three minutes in most human minds and hearts: the instinct to destroy what we perceive as the source of the problem. In that sense, he really is the "Savior of the World" (John 4:42) because that is the world's primary agenda, which he unmasks and then resolves with a quite different agenda. (p. 161)

- What is your response to Fr. Richard's definition here of how Jesus is the "Savior of the World"? In what ways does it align with your understanding? In what ways does it contradict or reshape your understanding?
- How can you begin to align yourself with Jesus's "quite different agenda" around violence?

28. Reflection

Jesus will speak critically against his own group whenever they try to use his message for oppositional thinking or group arrogance, or to justify violence. How different Christian history would have been had we listened to him!

The only thing more dangerous than the individual ego is the group ego. That's why, when Jesus calls the apostles, he immediately calls into question the two sacred institutions inside a Semitic culture—or most cultures, for that matter: job and family. (p. 162)

- When have you used Jesus's message for "oppositional thinking or group arrogance, or to justify violence"? Imagine what he would say to you about this. How would you respond?
- When have you been impacted by the dangerousness of a group ego? What response were you able to give at the time? What would you say or do now, especially if you could be protected from any consequences?
- What do you think Jesus would have to say about your attitudes toward job and family?

29. Reflection

My lifetime of studying Jesus would lead me to summarize all his teaching inside of two prime ideas: *forgiveness and inclusion*. Don't take my word for it; just go through the Gospels, story by story. It is rather self-evident. Forgiveness and inclusion are Jesus's great themes. They are the practical name of love—for without forgiveness and inclusivity, love is largely a sentimental valentine. They are also the two practices that most undercut human violence. (p. 163)

- Define forgiveness and inclusivity in your own words. Describe how you can imagine these practices undercutting violence.

- Recall a time when you have been genuinely forgiven by another person for something you have done or left undone. How did you feel about being forgiven? How did that act impact the relationship?

- Recall a time when you were graciously included by another person in a group or event. How did you feel about being included? How did that act impact your perspective and relationships with that group?

30. Reflection

I believe Jesus is teaching us that *if we put our energy into choosing the good—instead of the negative and largely illusionary energy of rejecting the bad—we will overcome evil in a much better way and will not become evil ourselves.* This is exactly what he does on the cross, and that is what gives me the courage to believe this is at the heart of his message. At our center in New Mexico, we have taken it as one of our central axioms that "the best criticism of the bad is the practice of the better." (p. 164)

- Where in your life do you most need to be "choosing the good" right now? What impact would this have on your life, your faith, and your relationships?

- Why would you imagine Fr. Richard thinks courage is necessary for believing and living from this viewpoint?

- How can you live out Fr. Richard's axiom that "the best criticism of the bad is the practice of the better"?

31. Reflection

The killing of Jesus is a judgment on how blind we *all* can be when we are enjoying the perks and privileges of power. Bad power, which *always* eliminates its opponents, killed Jesus. In Jesus's lifetime, that bad power was exercised by both Roman Empire and Jewish high priests, but we can change the names to fit every age and every culture.

That's how deep, unconscious, and irrational the scapegoat mechanism seems to be. (p. 165)

- In what ways do you enjoy "the perks and privileges of power"? What do you think Jesus would say about it? How would you respond?

- When have you witnessed the elimination of opponents by those in power—whether figuratively or literally? What did that experience teach you about living in Western society today?

- Spend some time in prayer, reflecting on what you've learned about the scapegoat mechanism. Describe in your journal what you've learned and how it has influenced your understanding and experience of your faith.

32. Contemplative Sit

Leading in with the quotation below, practice a contemplative sit. You may wish to set a timer or digital prayer bell for fifteen, twenty, or twenty-five minutes, so that you know when to finish.

- Seat yourself in a quiet area.

- Ground yourself and allow your breathing to settle.

- Notice any tightness in your shoulders and neck and allow any tension in your muscles to relax.

- Allow your back to rest in an aligned, neutral position.

- Once you are settled, read the following passage aloud—
  this is the opening text for your sit:

The powers-that-be know that nonviolent prophets...are a much deeper problem because they refuse to buy into the very illusions upon which the whole empire is built, especially the myth of redemptive violence. (p. 165)

- Continue your sit in silence—focusing on your breath, connecting with your body, or by practicing any other method with which you are familiar.
- Allow thoughts, feelings, and sensations to arise, exist, and then fall away while you keep your attention open and large, connecting to that much deeper consciousness.
- Remember, there is no goal. There is no right or wrong way—simply *be* present to what *is* in the moment.

Once finished, you may wish to journal your reflections on this experience.

CHAPTER EIGHT

The Resented Banquet

1. Contemplative Sit

Leading in with the quotation below, practice a contemplative sit. You may wish to set a timer or digital prayer bell for fifteen, twenty, or twenty-five minutes, so that you know when to finish.

- Seat yourself in a quiet area.
- Ground yourself and allow your breathing to settle.
- Notice any tightness in your shoulders and neck and allow any tension in your muscles to relax.
- Allow your back to rest in an aligned, neutral position.
- Once you are settled, read the following passage aloud— this is the opening text for your sit:

The central positive theme of the Bible . . . is the divine unmerited generosity that is everywhere available, totally given, usually unde-tected as such, and often even undesired. It is called grace. (p. 167)

- Continue your sit in silence—focusing on your breath, connecting with your body, or by practicing any other method with which you are familiar.
- Allow thoughts, feelings, and sensations to arise, exist, and then fall away while you keep your attention open and large, connecting to that much deeper consciousness.
- Remember, there is no goal. There is no right or wrong way—simply *be* present to what *is* in the moment.

Once finished, you may wish to journal your reflections on this experience.

2. Reflection

In the parable of the watchful servants (Luke 12:35–40), God is actually presented as *waiting on us*—in the middle of the night! In fact, God is presented as both our personal servant inside of our house, and a "burglar" who "breaks through the walls of that house." That's really quite extraordinary and not our usual image of God at all. That is how much God wants to get to us, and how unrelenting is the work of grace. (p. 168)

- How does it feel to have Fr. Richard describe God as a personal servant? What aspects of God does this image bring to mind? What stereotypes of God does it reinforce or demolish?
- How does it feel to have Fr. Richard describe God as a burglar? What aspects of God does this image bring to mind? What stereotypes of God does it reinforce or demolish?
- Write down your definition of grace. How does this paragraph alter that definition?

3. Reflection

Grace cannot be understood by any ledger of merits and demerits. It cannot be held to any patterns of buying, losing, earning, achieving, or manipulating, which is where, unfortunately, most of us live our lives. Grace is, quite literally, "for the taking." It is God eternally giving away God—for nothing, except the giving itself. (p. 168)

- What were you taught about God's "ledger of merits and demerits"? What role have such ideas played in your spiritual life?

- Which pattern(s) ("buying, losing, earning, achieving, or manipulating") have been most influential in your life and why?
- What feelings come to mind as you read the final two sentences of this passage?
- When have you glimpsed God giving away God in your life? What happened, and how did you respond?

4. Reflection

The ego does not know how to receive things freely or without logic. It prefers a worldview of scarcity, or at least quid pro quo, where only the clever win. It likes to be worthy and needs to understand in order to be able to accept things. That problem, and its overcoming, is at the very center of the Gospel plot line. It has always been overcome from God's side. The only problem is getting us in on the process! (p. 169)

- What were you taught about abundance and scarcity in your family of origin? What role have such ideas played in your spiritual life?
- What does it mean to you to be "worthy"? Describe the impact that concept has had on your life.
- Have you ever received anything completely for free—without any strings attached? Did you believe it? How did you feel?

5. Reflection

The early code words that become the awesome theme of grace are *banquet* and *food*....

Jesus opens up a new tradition of common and open table fellowship, including both a bread-and-fish tradition that seems to have fallen into disuse ("potluck suppers" for all, as alluded to in 1 Corinthians 11:17-34, and the multiplication stories in the Gospels) and a bread-and-wine tradition that was preserved as the Eucharist we now enjoy (but has largely been used to define membership and worthiness). (p. 169)

- What are your feelings about and experience with the Eucharist or Holy Communion? How have they changed over the course of your life?

- When have you witnessed the Eucharist being "used to define membership and worthiness"? What was your response?

- What are your feelings about and experience with potluck suppers? Is the idea of equating them with "the multiplication stories in the Gospels" new to you, or not? What is your response to this idea? How does it fit with your reading of the gospel stories—or not?

6. Reflection

It takes us a long time to be willing to come to the banquet (Luke 14:23; Matthew 22:4–6). *Strangely enough, in real life, people have tended to resent it, fear it, deny it, and make it impossible or difficult to attend. We are either afraid or unwilling to just celebrate the feast of divine union.* (p. 170)

- Read Luke 14:16–23. What would keep you from coming to the banquet—resentment, fear, denial, something else? What makes it hard for you to believe in such a gratuitous possibility?

- What stops you from believing that God would provide such a banquet every day of your life? How might you pray for a change of heart or a shift in perspective?

- Have you met people who seem to believe and live as if

such a banquet exists? What about them attracts you? What holds you back from becoming one of them?

7. Reflection

The Gospel needs to present humankind with a worldview of abundance instead of scarcity, a vision of grace instead of fear, of Holy Thursday baking day instead of Monday laundry day. But, so very sadly for the vast majority of Christians, a laundry day of purity codes has seemed to suffice. (p. 171)

- What do you think makes purity codes preferable to gratuitous abundance? Why do you think many Christians are so afraid of unmerited gifts?
- What would it take for you to embrace "a worldview of abundance instead of scarcity"? What holds you back?

8. Reflection

Even much of the European Reformation strikes me as guilt-based and not joy-encountered. Like nothing else, it perhaps explains the dour, dutiful, and often resentful character of so much civil religion. Such a passive-aggressive stance toward reality will never invite or change the world....

That's what grace does. It empowers those who really love and trust God and, frankly, leaves all others in the realm of missed opportunity. Our image for that missed opportunity has been a later hell, but it is primarily and clearly an emptiness now. (p. 171)

- What is your experience with "guilt-based...dour, dutiful, and often resentful" religion? What attracts and/or repels you in such a religion? What do you imagine attracts others to it?

- What is your perspective on the idea of hell? How would you describe it to someone who hasn't heard of it before? How does it feel to have Fr. Richard equate hell with "missed opportunity" and "emptiness now"?

9. Reflection

As long as we remain inside of a win-lose script, Christianity will continue to appeal to low-level and self-interested morality and never rise to the mystical banquet that Jesus really offers us. It will be duty instead of delight, "jars of purification" (John 2:6) instead of one-hundred-fifty gallons of intoxicating wine at the end of the party (John 2:7–10). How did we avoid missing the clear message on that one? (p. 172)

- How would you define your morality? How does it compare with what Fr. Richard outlines here?
- Describe "the mystical banquet that Jesus really offers us." Why does Fr. Richard believe we need to "rise" to that level?
- Explain Fr. Richard's "clear message" of this paragraph in your own words.

10. Reflection

The game that I call "meritocracy" is really found in almost all cultures, insofar as I can tell. Maybe culture could even be defined as attempts to "earn worthiness" or to validate the self by some extrinsic measure. This is the dead-ended mentality that made Jesus, as John's Gospel puts it (2:15), "create a whip of cords" and go to the temple to destroy the system of buying and selling. Why? Because until that mind is somehow changed, we *cannot* understand the Gospel. (p. 173)

- How has meritocracy shaped your life? In what ways has the goal of "worthiness" influenced your understanding of God's love?
- Read John 2:13–16. What has been your understanding of this story? In what ways has Fr. Richard changed or challenged that understanding?
- What do you imagine it would be like to have your mind "somehow changed"? Would you be willing to pray for such significant change in your perspective? What might you gain or lose in embracing such a radically different understanding of the Gospel?

11. Reflection

Buying and selling invariably takes over the temple itself. It defeats the essential work of religion—at least as Jesus understood religion. It obviously made Jesus quite angry. If there is any violence in Jesus's life, this is it, but he directs it toward attempts to "buy" God. His violence is not against people, but against self-serving religion and its frequent alliance with power and money.

Also, I am sure, Jesus is quite angry at any attempt to "buy" God's love or to make religion into an exclusive club, which is shown by the overtly inclusive quote that he takes from Isaiah: "My house is to be a house of prayer for *all the peoples*" (56:7). (p. 173)

- In what ways have you seen "buying and selling invariably take over" the church? How does this affect your feelings about the value of "buying and selling" in general?
- When have you attempted to "buy" God's love? What did you do and what was the result? How do you want to reframe your understanding of God's love as a result of reading *Things Hidden*?

- What change(s) would have to occur for your church to "be a house of prayer for *all the peoples*"?

12. Reflection

Parables aim to subvert our old consciousness and offer us a way through by utterly reframing our worldview.

So often, the biblical text is not a transformative document and does not bring about a "new creation" because we pull it inside of our own security systems and what we call "common sense." At that point, no divine breakthrough is possible. Frankly speaking, much of Scripture, then, has become largely harmless and forgettable. (p. 174)

- Which of Jesus's parables has most shifted your worldview? When and how did that happen?
- Which of Jesus's parables have caused you the most trouble? Why?
- Which of Jesus's parables is the most difficult to explain to others? Why?
- How attached are you to "common sense"? What does it take for you to be open to a "new creation"?

13. Reflection

With Constantine's Edict of Milan in 313, both grace and forgiveness basically became politicized and controlled by formula and technique. *They became juridical concepts instead of spiritual realizations....*

Sin management became the work of the priesthood much more than the marvelous work of transformation and inner realization that we see in Jesus's ministry. (pp. 174–175)

- Describe the role of the priesthood in your own words. Reflect on which aspects of tradition and teaching inform this view.

- Describe Jesus's ministry and contrast it with the role of the priesthood you outlined above. What do you notice?
- What would it mean in your life if "grace and forgiveness" could clearly lead you into "the marvelous work of transformation and inner realization"?

14. Reflection

When forgiveness becomes largely a juridical process, then we who are in charge can measure it out, define who's in and who's out, and determine ways to earn it and exclude the unworthy. *It makes for good religion, but not for good spirituality at all.* We have destroyed the likelihood that most people will ever experience the pure gift of God's forgiveness. We have pushed people away from God, whose forgiveness cannot be earned by any technique whatsoever. It is only and always received as a pure gift—and that is *precisely* the experience that changes us so deeply. Otherwise, it is not grace. (p. 175)

- In what ways have you experienced forgiveness as "largely a juridical process"? How has this influenced your concept of God's love?
- Explain Fr. Richard's statement that a juridical process *"makes for good religion, but not for good spirituality at all."*
- When have you experienced God's forgiveness as "pure gift"? What did you gain from that experience?

15. Reflection

At least 80 percent of people's operative God images are a subtle combination of their mom and their dad or any other significant authority figures. Once they begin an inner life of prayer and in-depth study of sacred texts, that slowly begins to change. From then on, it only gets better and better. Grace does its work and creates a "work of art" (Ephesians 2:10). (p. 176)

- What impact did your mother and/or other female-identi-fied parental figures have on your image of God? How and why has this changed over the years?
- What impact did your father and/or other male-identified parental figures have on your image of God? How and why has this changed over the years?
- What other authority figures have influenced your image of God, and in what ways? How and why has this changed over the years?

16. *Lectio* Practice

The miracle of grace and true prayer is that they invade the unconscious mind and heart. They invade them so much that the love of God and the love of self invariably proceed forward together. On the practical level, they are experienced as the same thing! (p. 176)

Slowly read aloud the quotation above four times, following these instructions.

1. With the first reading of the text, allow yourself to *settle in* to the exercise and familiarize yourself with the words. Read the text out loud, very slowly and clearly. Pause for a breath or two before moving on.

2. For the second reading, *listen* from a centered heart space and notice any word or phrase that stands out to you.

3. After a few moments of silence, read the text a third time, *reflecting* on how this word or phrase is connected to your current life experience. Take a minute to linger over this word or phrase

and allow it to engage your body, heart, and awareness of the world around you.

You may want to speak a response aloud or write something in your journal.

4. For the final reading, *respond* with a prayer or expression of what you have experienced, inviting the infinite wisdom of God to support you in places of unknowing, confusion, desire, or hope.

17. Reflection

The whole movement of the Bible is toward the possibility of intimacy, divine union, full personhood, and there has to be some degree of *sameness* for that to happen. I will keep repeating that, so you will know the tangent and will be ready for God's solution. (pp. 176–177)

- What would it mean for you to have "intimacy" with God? What thoughts and feelings arise as you consider this possibility?
- What might "divine union" with God look like for you? What thoughts and feelings arise as you consider this possibility?
- In what ways have you developed "some degree of *sameness*" with God over the course of your life? What has this meant for your relationship with God?

18. Reflection

From the very beginning, Divine election is utterly free, gratuitous, and indifferent to any criterion of worthiness. It never has been a worthiness contest, and God's favor never will be earned. This is very hard for almost everybody to accept. It just does not compute. (p. 177)

- In what ways have you tried to earn God's love over the course of your life? How has that worked out for you? How has it influenced your view of yourself, others, and God?

- What would it be like for you to let go of "any criterion of worthiness" in your relationship with God? What thoughts and feelings arise as you consider this possibility? What would need to change for you to embrace this idea?

- What still "does not compute" from what you're reading in *Things Hidden*? How might you take that to prayer?

19. Contemplative Sit

Leading in with the quotation below, practice a contemplative sit. You may wish to set a timer or digital prayer bell for fifteen, twenty, or twenty-five minutes, so that you know when to finish.

- Seat yourself in a quiet area.

- Ground yourself and allow your breathing to settle.

- Notice any tightness in your shoulders and neck and allow any tension in your muscles to relax.

- Allow your back to rest in an aligned, neutral position.

- Once you are settled, read the following passage aloud— this is the opening text for your sit:

"God does not love us because we are good; God loves us because God is good." (p. 177)

- Continue your sit in silence—focusing on your breath, connecting with your body, or by practicing any other method with which you are familiar.

- Allow thoughts, feelings, and sensations to arise, exist, and then fall away while you keep your attention open and large, connecting to that much deeper consciousness.

- Remember, there is no goal. There is no right or wrong way—simply *be* present to what *is* in the moment.

Once finished, you may wish to journal your reflections on this experience.

20. Reflection

God makes use of everything that we offer and seems most grateful for the tiniest bit of connection from our side. This is the faith desire that is needed, and even important, from us. Otherwise, it would not be a covenant, but rather a coercion. There is no evidence that Jesus heals worthy people. He does heal desirous people, but God even creates that desire! (pp. 177–178)

- What is your response to Fr. Richard's statement that "God makes use of everything that we offer"? When have you witnessed or experienced this? What did it teach you about being in relationship with God?
- Describe your understanding of a covenant. How has your reading of *Things Hidden* changed or expanded that understanding?
- Why is it important, even required, that we desire relationship with God? What does it mean that God "creates that desire" within us?

21. Reflection

David is the archetypal whole person of the Hebrew Scriptures, even psychologically, yet his "holiness" is totally created by God's involvement with him. He's the violent warrior (2 Samuel 8–10). He's the adulterer who impregnates a married woman and the egocentric leader who allows Uriah to be killed to protect his own name (2 Samuel 11). (p. 178)

- What does it mean for you that someone as violent and immoral as David is called by God and made holy? What does it mean for the people in your circle (family, friends, church members, etc.)?

- How has God's involvement in your life made you more holy? What thoughts and feelings arise as you consider this question?

22. Reflection

David, like all of us on the spiritual path, eventually realizes that whatever worthiness he has is entirely a gift. God implants a bit of the Godself in us, called the Holy Spirit (Romans 5:5, 8:9–10; 1 Corinthians 3:16–17), and God *cannot not* love what God sees there. Paul even calls our very bodies "temples" (1 Corinthians 6:19). God has created just enough equality to make a covenant of love possible. (p. 179)

- What is your gut-level response to reading that "God implants a bit of the Godself in us, called the Holy Spirit"? To what extent can you believe this is true? In what ways have you experienced this truth in your life—or not?

- What was your understanding of and/or relationship with the Holy Spirit prior to reading *Things Hidden*? In what ways has this changed over your time of working with this Companion Guide?

- How did your body respond to reading that "Paul even calls our very bodies 'temples'"? In what ways have you treated your body as a temple, and in what ways have you not? How has that treatment impacted your ability to believe and receive Paul's message? What changes might you like to make in how you treat your body?

23. Reflection

To paraphrase Meister Eckhart, the love by which we think we are loving God is actually the love by which God first loved us. All we are doing is completing the circuit and allowing the flow (see John 15:16). We cannot really get there; we can only be there. God does all the loving. (p. 179)

- How does it feel to read that "God does all the loving"? What questions or certainties arise in you as you consider this idea?
- When in your life have you experienced a moment of "completing the circuit and allowing the flow"? How did it affect your concept of love and your willingness to love?
- If "God does all the loving," what does that say about our desire for control in our relationships, with others and with God? What feelings arise as you ponder this question?

24. Contemplative Sit

Leading in with the quotation below, practice a contemplative sit. You may wish to set a timer or digital prayer bell for fifteen, twenty, or twenty-five minutes, so that you know when to finish.

- Seat yourself in a quiet area.
- Ground yourself and allow your breathing to settle.
- Notice any tightness in your shoulders and neck and allow any tension in your muscles to relax.
- Allow your back to rest in an aligned, neutral position.
- Once you are settled, read the following passage aloud— this is the opening text for your sit:

The dualistic mind cannot access union, wholeness, eternity, or holiness. Only God in me can know God, only love can recognize love, only union can enjoy union. (pp. 179–180)

- Continue your sit in silence—focusing on your breath, connecting with your body, or by practicing any other method with which you are familiar.
- Allow thoughts, feelings, and sensations to arise, exist, and then fall away while you keep your attention open and large, connecting to that much deeper consciousness.
- Remember, there is no goal. There is no right or wrong way—simply *be* present to what *is* in the moment.

Once finished, you may wish to journal your reflections on this experience.

25. Reflection

The moment we become whole and holy is when we can accept our shadow self or, to put it in moral language, that is when we can admit our sin. *Basically, we move from unconsciousness to consciousness by a deliberate struggle with our shadow self.* Jesus himself only begins to speak after he has been "led by the Spirit...to be tempted by the devil" (Matthew 4:1)....Only then do we "awaken." (p. 180)

- When have you been "tempted by the devil"? What happened, how did you respond, and what was the result of your response at the time? What is your assessment today of the impact of that event on your life and your relationship with God?
- What, if anything, do you recall about moments of moving *"from unconsciousness to consciousness"*? What struggles with the shadow self precipitated those movements? What transformations have occurred in your life as a result?
- In what ways do you believe you are awake today? What are the fruits of that awakened state in your life?

26. Reflection

God seems quite practiced in using people's sin for good, but God cannot use those who refuse to see their dark side. *Jesus himself is never upset at sinners. He's only upset with people who don't think they are sinners.* Righteous folks are much more problematic for Jesus because they are only half there, at best. (p. 181)

- When have you refused to see your "dark side," even when others have pointed it out to you? What changed, then or later, to enable you to see that moment clearly now? Has God used that lesson in your life in some way?

- How do you feel about self-righteous people? What prayer might you say for them?

- In what ways are you self-righteous? What thoughts and feelings arise when you read that "God cannot use" you if you refuse to see your dark side?

27. Reflection

To allow ourselves to be God's beloved is to be God's beloved. To allow ourselves to be chosen is to be chosen. To allow ourselves to be blessed is to be blessed. It is so hard to accept being accepted, especially from God. It takes a certain kind of humility to surrender to it, and even more to persist in believing it. Any persons used by God know this to be true: God chooses and then uses whom God chooses, and their usability comes from their willingness to allow themselves to be chosen in the first place. What a paradox! (p. 182)

- What are your feelings about allowing others to do things for you? How is this similar to or different from allowing God to love you? Which is more difficult and why?

- Explain why Fr. Richard states, "It takes a certain kind of humility to surrender to it, and even more to persist in believing it."
- In what ways are you usable by God? In what ways are you unwilling to be used by God? What do you resist or fear?

28. Activity and Reflection

In this marvelous early affirmation...are found five generous and glorious adjectives that describe the heart and soul of Israel's belief. Somehow, against all odds and neighbors, they were able to experience a God who was merciful (in Hebrew, *rhm*), compassionate/gracious *(hnn)*, steadfast in love *(hsd)*, tenaciously faithful *('emeth)*, and forgiving *(ns')*. (p. 183)

- List the "five generous and glorious adjectives" in your journal or on paper. Write down an example beside each adjective of when you have experienced or witnessed God acting in these ways. Then write down an example of when you have acted in these ways because of your relationship with God.
- Which of these adjectives is the easiest for you to believe in and why?
- Which of these adjectives is the hardest for you to believe in and why?
- Which of these adjectives is the easiest for you to act upon and why?
- Which of these adjectives is the hardest for you to act upon and why?

29. Reflection

The word that is translated as "steadfast love" is often rendered "covenant love" or "faithful love." Today, we often call it unconditional love.

It's "one-sided love," if you will, because Israel never, never keeps its side of the covenant, just as we never keep our side of the relationship to this day. Yahweh has recognized that everything must be done from God's side. That is the constant and relentless message of much of the Hebrew Scriptures. (p. 184)

- Re-read the different descriptions of God's love in this passage. Which one resonates with you the most and why? Which one is most difficult to comprehend and why?

- Do you agree with Fr. Richard's declaration that "Israel never, never keeps its side of the covenant"? Why or why not?

- Do you agree with Fr. Richard's declaration that "we never keep our side of the relationship to this day"? Why or why not?

- What thoughts and feelings arise for you when you read that "Yahweh has recognized that everything must be done from God's side"?

30. *Lectio* Practice

Yahweh's response to failure is *"I will love you at even deeper levels because I am determined to win.* Your pettiness is not going to determine or limit my greatness." (p. 185)

Slowly read aloud the quotation above four times, following these instructions.

1. With the first reading of the text, allow yourself to *settle in* to the exercise and familiarize yourself with the words. Read the text out loud, very slowly and clearly. Pause for a breath or two before moving on.

2. For the second reading, *listen* from a centered heart space and notice any word or phrase that stands out to you.

3. After a few moments of silence, read the text a third time, *reflecting* on how this word or phrase is connected to your current life experience. Take a minute to linger over this word or phrase and allow it to engage your body, heart, and awareness of the world around you.

You may want to speak a response aloud or write something in your journal.

4. For the final reading, *respond* with a prayer or expression of what you have experienced, inviting the infinite wisdom of God to support you in places of unknowing, confusion, desire, or hope.

31. Reflection

The gate of hell is always a door swinging both ways. No one is there unless they want to be, and anyone who wants more can always decide differently. But when I see how people resist and avoid change here, I can see why the Scriptures used the metaphor of a tragic and "eternal fire." The logical possibility of an eternal hell must be allowed, even though, interestingly, the church has never declared a single person to be there. (p. 186)

- How is Fr. Richard's description of hell similar and/or different from your own? How is your understanding of hell similar and/or different from others in your church community?
- What impact does the idea of hell have on the way you live your life?
- What would change for you if you believed that people could leave hell whenever they want?

32. Reflection

Good spiritual teachers always put a deliberate choice before their students, to call them to decision. Moses did so in his last days: "I set before you life or death, blessing or curse. Choose life!" (Deuteronomy 30:19)....

This theme will be continued in many of the prophets, in one form or another, including Jesus, who stated his radical alternatives as "God or money" (Matthew 6:24; Luke 16:13)....Prophetic choices are made to be quite black-and-white, intentionally dualistic, to force us to weigh the consequences, to be choiceful and conscious. (pp. 186–187)

- When has a spiritual teacher "put a deliberate choice" before you? What did you choose and why? What have been the consequences of that choice?
- When have you chosen life over death? What have been the consequences of that choice?
- When have you chosen money over God? What have been the consequences of that choice?
- When have you chosen God over money? What have been the consequences of that choice?

33. Reflection

Unfortunately, we made [metaphors such as hell] into *physical* places instead of descriptions of states of mind and heart and calls to decision *in this world*.... We pushed the whole thing off into the future and took it out of the now. Inasmuch as we did so, we lost the in-depth transformative power of the Christian religion. It became a soul-saving society for the next world instead of a healing of body, soul, and society now—and, therefore, forever! (pp. 187–188)

- What difference does it make in your understanding of hell to have Fr. Richard locate it as a state of mind and heart in the here-and-now? How does it impact your view of the society in which you live?

- In what ways have you made your life a living hell? How has that impacted your relationship with God and others?

- When have you chosen to walk away from a living hell? In what ways was that "a healing of body [and] soul"?

34. Reflection

For Jesus, *all rewards are inherent to the action itself and all punishments are inherent to the action itself*, but we largely pushed all rewards and punishments into the future....

What we choose now, we will have then. God is giving everyone exactly what they want. Mature religion creates an affinity, a connaturality, a kinship between this world and the next. One is not a testing ground for the next, but a "practicing" and choosing for the next. Christianity is quite simply *practicing for heaven*. (p. 188)

- Think of a time when a reward or punishment was inherent in your action. What happened and what was the result?

- What is your response to Fr. Richard's statement that "God is giving everyone exactly what they want"?

- What changes would you like to make in your life in response to the idea that you are now "practicing for heaven"?

35. Reflection

In the New Testament, and particularly in Jesus, the most common image for what God is offering us is a banquet. It's not a trophy, not a prize, not a reward later, but a participative and joyous party now.

A banquet has everything to do with invitation and acceptance; it is never a command performance. (p. 189)

- Before you read this paragraph, what did you think was "the most common image for what God is offering us"? What is your response to the idea that a banquet is the most common? What questions or revelations arise in you as you ponder this?
- Are you a party person? In what ways does this image work or not work for you?
- What is your response to the idea that God's invitation "is never a command performance"?

36. Reflection

At the end of the parable (Matthew 22:9–10), the king instructs the servants, "Go out and invite everyone to the wedding feast, the good and the bad alike." That phrase has been shocking to Christians from the very beginning. They didn't know how to compute it, precisely because they assumed that Jesus's message was primarily a moral matter in which "bad" people would clearly not belong. Once we know it is primarily a mystical matter, a realization of union, it reframes the entire journey. Almost by accident, we find ourselves becoming "moral," but our morality did not earn us a ticket to the banquet. (p. 190)

- To what extent have you believed that any banquet attendance is "primarily a moral matter"? How does your understanding of the banquet change in light of Fr. Richard framing it as "primarily a mystical matter"?
- In what ways do you try to "earn…a ticket to the banquet"? What would need to shift within you so you could accept that ticket as a free gift?
- What would it mean to you to be able to party with God?

37. Reflection

Jesus is always undercutting what we think is common sense. I don't think this passage is a call to love the poor as much as it is a call to think non-dualistically, to change our entire form of consciousness. "When you have a party, invite the poor, the crippled, the lame, the blind, because *the fact that they cannot pay you back will mean you are fortunate*" (Luke 14:13)—because now you are inside of a different mind that will allow you to read all your life from a worldview of abundance instead of a worldview of scarcity. That, by the way, *will* cause you to start loving the poor—almost naturally. (p. 191)

- In what ways is the paragraph above "undercutting" your previous reading of banquet Scripture passages? How does it transform your perspective on loving the poor?
- What would it feel like to believe you lived with enough abundance that you could invite all the poor to your dinner party without needing to worry about their ability to repay you in the future? What would need to shift within you for you to begin living *as if* that were true?

38. Reflection

Even the Eucharist has usually been presented as a reward system for good behavior, a worthiness contest, a sacrificial system. We often see it more as an agreed-upon belief system rather than as the simple, gratuitous table fellowship that it was for Jesus and his first unworthy followers. (p. 192)

- How has the Eucharist "been presented" to you over the course of your life? In what ways have you accepted those ideas? When and why might you have resisted or rebelled against any of those ideas?

- Do you consider yourself a worthy or unworthy follower of Jesus and why?
- What would need to change in the presentation of the Eucharist for you to believe it is "simple, gratuitous table fellowship"?

39. Reflection

All these dimensions [of Mary as an archetype] point to the full meaning of how God is born into the world. It is never about us, and always about God. We, like she, are merely "handmaids" (Luke 1:38) and instruments, and it took such a woman as this to make the whole pattern clear. (p. 193)

- What thoughts and feelings arise in you when you read "It is never about us, and always about God"? How does this viewpoint challenge and/or confirm what you've been taught about yourself?
- What are the attributes of a "handmaid" or an "instrument"? What would it be like to cultivate some of those attributes in yourself?

40. Reflection

Now, notice that the word *favor* doesn't say anything about *her*. Favor says something about the one who is doing the favoring, so it's really not saying anything about Mary. It's saying something about God's election of Mary. She is one who is the absolutely perfect receiver, and refuses to play the "Lord, I am not worthy" card that had become normative in most biblical theophanies. She just says, "Let it be done unto me" (Luke 1:38). (p. 194)

- Describe your understanding of and attitude toward Mary. How has what you're reading in this chapter of *Things Hidden* influenced or shifted that understanding?

- What characteristics would make someone "the absolutely perfect receiver"? Think about the characteristics you've been taught to apply to Mary. In what ways do these characteristics align or conflict?
- What would make you a better "receiver"? What would it take for you to be willing to say, "Let it be done unto me"?

41. *Lectio* Practice

We don't know how to say yes by ourselves. We just "second the motion." *There is a part of us, the Holy Spirit within, that has always said yes to God.* God first says "yes" inside of us and we say, "Oh yeah," thinking it comes from us. In other words, God rewards us for letting God reward us. Think about that, maybe even for the rest of your life. (p. 195)

Slowly read aloud the quotation above four times, following these instructions.

1. With the first reading of the text, allow yourself to *settle in* to the exercise and familiarize yourself with the words. Read the text out loud, very slowly and clearly. Pause for a breath or two before moving on.

2. For the second reading, *listen* from a centered heart space and notice any word or phrase that stands out to you.

3. After a few moments of silence, read the text a third time, *reflecting* on how this word or phrase is connected to your current life experience. Take a minute to linger over this word or phrase and allow it to engage your body, heart, and awareness of the world around you.

You may want to speak a response aloud or write something in your journal.

4. For the final reading, *respond* with a prayer or expression of what you have experienced, inviting the infinite wisdom of God to support you in places of unknowing, confusion, desire, or hope.

42. Reflection

The banquet begins.... Course after course, Babette lays on the table an enormous, beautiful, sumptuous feast. The guests' eyes just widen, but as they drink a little more and more of the wine, they loosen up. They learn, finally, to enjoy this banquet that they never thought they could possibly enjoy. It was a world into which no one had ever invited them. (pp. 197–198)

- Revisit your reflections on the idea of banquets earlier in this chapter (Reflections 6–9, 25, 36). Then re-read Fr. Richard's description of Babette's feast (pp. 196–200). What do you notice and what connections do you make?
- What helps you to "loosen up"? What unmerited gifts from God have enabled your eyes to widen and your soul and body to enjoy something unexpected?
- If the angel Gabriel showed up and said, "Hail, favored one," (p. 193) how would you respond and why?

43. Activity

Babette wins the lottery: ten thousand francs. After some negotiation, she talks the sisters into allowing her to prepare a fine French banquet to celebrate their deceased father's one hundredth anniversary of birth. (p. 197)

Imagine you've won the lottery and you want to prepare a banquet. Prayerfully ponder the following questions:

- Who would you invite and why? What special occasion might you use to encourage them to attend? Could you do this without expecting anything in return, other than your guests' enjoyment of the banquet?

- Where would you host it and why? What sort of venue would you choose: home or away, indoors or out, city or countryside? What season, what theme, what amenities would you want?

- What would you serve and why? Consider each dish for its taste, meaning, value, and importance. (It wouldn't matter whether you could cook them because you can hire your own Babette if you prefer not to cook!)

- How would you decorate and why? What kind of mood do you want to set for this occasion? Is it a black-tie event, a costume ball, or a family style get-together with an evening of storytelling? What types of centerpieces, small gifts, and/or unusual artwork would bring meaning and enjoyment for your guests?

- What auxiliary spaces, such as a kids' table, a quiet room, a dance floor, or other meaningful areas would you incorporate into your banquet? What would help those you have invited feel even more comfortable and happy?

- What entertainment would you provide? Would there be a poetry reading, a comedy act, games, or a floor show? What types of music would you choose for each section of the evening/day/weekend and why?

- In what other ways could you share your newfound abundance with these precious people?

Take some time in silence to give thanks to God for the abundance of spirit which allowed you to imagine these possibilities. Then ask yourself the following question:

What would it be like to plan a small-scale version of this event as God's gift to you? Perhaps you might just gather one or two people, serve one or two special foods, arrange a lovely centerpiece, find the right music online. What feelings arise as you consider this possibility?

44. Contemplative Sit

Leading in with the quotation below, practice a contemplative sit. You may wish to set a timer or digital prayer bell for fifteen, twenty, or twenty-five minutes, so that you know when to finish.

- Seat yourself in a quiet area.
- Ground yourself and allow your breathing to settle.
- Notice any tightness in your shoulders and neck and allow any tension in your muscles to relax.
- Allow your back to rest in an aligned, neutral position.
- Once you are settled, read the following passage aloud—this is the opening text for your sit:

We all find ourselves with this surprising ability to love God and to desire love from God, often for no reason in particular. That doesn't happen every day, truly, but hopefully arises more often as we learn to trust and rest in life. Moments of unconditional love sort of slip out of us and no one is more surprised when they happen. But when they do, we always know we are living inside of a Larger Life than our own. We know, henceforth, that our life is not about us, but we are about God. (pp. 195–196)

- Continue your sit in silence—focusing on your breath, connecting with your body, or by practicing any other method with which you are familiar.

- Allow thoughts, feelings, and sensations to arise, exist, and then fall away while you keep your attention open and large, connecting to that much deeper consciousness.
- Remember, there is no goal. There is no right or wrong way—simply *be* present to what *is* in the moment.

Once finished, you may wish to journal your reflections on this experience.

CHAPTER NINE

The Mystery of the Cross

1. Contemplative Sit

Leading in with the quotation below, practice a contemplative sit. You may wish to set a timer or digital prayer bell for twenty or twenty-five minutes, so that you know when to finish.

- Seat yourself in a quiet area.
- Ground yourself and allow your breathing to settle.
- Notice any tightness in your shoulders and neck and allow any tension in your muscles to relax.
- Allow your back to rest in an aligned, neutral position.
- Once you are settled, read the following passage aloud—this is the opening text for your sit:

Those who "gaze upon" (John 19:37) the crucified long enough—with contemplative eyes—are always healed at deep levels of pain, unforgiveness, aggressivity, and victimhood. (p. 202)

- Continue your sit in silence—focusing on your breath, connecting with your body, or by practicing any other method with which you are familiar.
- Allow thoughts, feelings, and sensations to arise, exist, and then fall away while you keep your attention open and large, connecting to that much deeper consciousness.
- Remember, there is no goal. There is no right or wrong way—simply *be* present to what *is* in the moment.

Once finished, you may wish to journal your reflections on this experience.

2. Reflection

Once we see the crucifixion event as an iconic symbol clarifying the very nature of God, the core human dilemma, and the essential religious agenda, we can see how true the statement ["the cross proves everything"] is....

For many people with whom I have worked, the crucified Jesus is no stranger to their souls at all. It had little to do with the traditional atonement theories and everything to do with their inner lives, and their attempts to make sense out of the tragic history of the world. The mystery of Jesus crucified *names* and *releases* the lives and even the deaths of many who live on our planet. (pp. 201–202)

- Describe your understanding of the importance of the crucified Jesus. How has this understanding changed over the course of your life?
- What are your feelings about the crucified Jesus? How does his crucifixion relate and compare to other elements of his life?
- Which teachings about the crucified Jesus have been most problematic for you and why?
- Which teachings about the crucified Jesus have been most important and/or powerful for you and why?
- Describe in your own words what you think Fr. Richard means by his final sentence in the paragraph above.

3. Reflection

The mystery of the rejection, suffering, passion, death, and raising up of Jesus is *the interpretative key* for what history means and where it is all going. Without such cosmic meaning and soul significance, the agonies and tragedies of humanity feel like Shakespeare's "sound and fury signifying nothing." The body can live without food more easily than the soul can live without such meaning. (p. 202)

- What is your response to reading this paragraph? What feelings or questions arise in you?
- Where have you found meaning in life? How has that changed over time?
- If you can do this safely, remember a time when you felt that "the agonies and tragedies of humanity" did signify nothing? Where and how and with whom did you find hope? What role, if any, did the crucified Jesus have in that process?

4. Reflection

If God is somehow participating in human suffering, instead of just passively tolerating it and observing it, that also changes everything—at least for those who are willing to "gaze" contemplatively.

We Christians are given the privilege to *name* the mystery rightly and to know it directly and consciously. (pp. 202–203)

- What does it mean to you that God is with us in our suffering? What questions does it raise or answer?
- How does it feel to have Fr. Richard label this a "mystery"? What questions does it raise or answer?
- Why and how could it "change everything" to gaze contemplatively on another's suffering?

5. Reflection

Enslavement and exodus are the great Jewish lenses through which history is read.

Add to that the story of Job, who unjustly but trustfully suffered and was restored (Job 42:9–17), and the four "Servant Songs" of Isaiah 42–53, whose central figure suffers in a way that is vicarious, redemptive, and life-giving for others. The Jewish psyche and expectations are gradually formed by these stories and images. Clearly, they were known by Jesus, and he evidently sees himself as representing this pattern, as revealed in his talks with his disciples. (pp. 203–204)

- What role have the themes of slavery, freedom, and unjust suffering played in the formation of your own "psyche and expectations"? What related stories and images come to mind for you?
- When have you suffered in a way that felt unjust? What happened and how did you overcome it or live through it? What did you learn from that experience and how did it impact your concept of and relationship with God and Jesus?

6. Reflection

The theological term for this classic pattern of descent and ascent was coined by Saint Augustine as "the paschal mystery." We now proclaim it publicly at every Eucharist as "*the* mystery of faith"!

So how does this happen? How does the victim transform us? How does the Lamb of God "take away" our sin (John 1:29), to use the common metaphor? How does Jesus "overcome death and darkness," as we often say? Is it just a heavenly transaction on God's side, or is it more an *agenda that God gives us for our side?* (p. 204)

- Have you ever pondered or tried to explain "*the* mystery of faith" or have you taken that phrase for granted as part of the Eucharistic language? What new thoughts and feelings came to you when Fr. Richard explained the phrase?

- Respond to Fr. Richard's questions to the best of your ability. What do you notice in your responses? What further questions arise?

7. Reflection

Jesus is saying, in effect: *This is how evil is transformed into good. I am going to take the worst thing and turn it into the best thing, so you will never be victimized, destroyed, or helpless again. I am giving YOU the victory over all death!* (pp. 204–205)

- What is your felt response to Fr. Richard's declaration?
- What thoughts come to you in response to Fr. Richard's declaration?
- What do you wonder or worry about after reading this paragraph?

8. Reflection

Jesus on the cross identifies with the human problem, the sin, the darkness. He refuses to stand above or outside the human dilemma. Further, he refuses to be the scapegoater, and instead becomes the scapegoat personified. In Paul's language, "Christ redeemed us from the curse…by being cursed himself" (Galatians 3:13); or "God made the sinless one into sin, so that in him [together with him!] we might become the very goodness of God" (2 Corinthians 5:21). Wow! Just gaze upon that mystery for a few years. (p. 206)

- What does it mean for you that Jesus was willing and able to both join in "the human dilemma" and refuse to scapegoat it in some way? What does that tell you about the nature of God in Christ?
- What is your response to Paul's declaration that "we might become the very goodness of God"? Is there some part of that mystery that you can articulate in any way, or not?

9. Contemplative Sit

Leading in with the quotation below, practice a contemplative sit. You may wish to set a timer or digital prayer bell for twenty or twenty-five minutes, so that you know when to finish.

- Seat yourself in a quiet area.
- Ground yourself and allow your breathing to settle.
- Notice any tightness in your shoulders and neck and allow any tension in your muscles to relax.
- Allow your back to rest in an aligned, neutral position.
- Once you are settled, read the following passage aloud—this is the opening text for your sit:

Evil is not overcome by attack or even avoidance, but by union at a higher level. It is overcome not by right or might, but rather by fusion! (p. 206)

- Continue your sit in silence—focusing on your breath, connecting with your body, or by practicing any other method with which you are familiar.
- Allow thoughts, feelings, and sensations to arise, exist, and then fall away while you keep your attention open and large, connecting to that much deeper consciousness.
- Remember, there is no goal. There is no right or wrong way—simply *be* present to what *is* in the moment.

Once finished, you may wish to journal your reflections on this experience.

10. Reflection

The victim state has been the plight of most people who have ever lived on this earth, so in all three cases we see Jesus identifying with humanity at its most critical and vulnerable level. It is God in solidarity with the pain of the world, it seems, much more than the Omnipotent One who, with a flick of the hand, overcomes all pain. (p. 206)

- How does it feel for you to imagine Jesus willingly taking on "the victim state"? What would you say to him about that if he were sitting next to you right now?

- If you can do this in a safe manner, recall a time when you felt vulnerable and/or victimized. If this becomes too painful for you, move to the next reflection. Were you aware of Jesus with you at the time? Can you imagine "God being in solidarity" with your pain through Jesus right now? What impact does that have on your memory and/or your thoughts about that event?

- Is omnipotence an important attribute of God for you? What impact does this reading have on your understanding of God's omnipotence and power?

11. Reflection

In the Passover commemoration, we have an image of the death of something good, innocent, and even loved.

What could that symbolize? I personally think it is an image of the ego, or the false self, which always feels good, adequate, and even innocent. What has to die is not something that looks evil, but, in fact, something that feels like "me"!... *It is these seemingly essential and good things that break us through into much deeper levels of life—when we let them go!* (p. 207)

- What "*seemingly essential and good things*" have you had to let go of in your life? What did you think and/or fear about letting them go? What happened when you did let go? How do you feel about that process now?

- Spend some time in prayer about what elements of the ego or false self might be holding you back. What is it time to let go of and why?

12. Reflection

To understand Jesus in a whole new way, we must first know that *Christ* is not his last name, but his transformed identity after the Resurrection—which takes humanity and all of creation along in its sweet path. Jesus *became* the Christ, and he included us in this identity.

That's why Paul will create the new term "the Body of Christ," which clearly includes all of us. (p. 208)

- What has been your understanding about the names *Jesus* and *Christ*? What new or enlarging aspects has Fr. Richard revealed to you here? What difference does this make in how you view the second person of the Trinity?
- What does it mean that you *belong* in "the Body of Christ"? What would you like to do with that new "identity"?
- What does it mean that everyone else also belongs in "the Body of Christ"? How does that alter your understanding of community and society?

13. Reflection

I would ask you to consider the crucifix as a *homeopathic* image, like those medicines that give you just enough of the disease so you can develop a resistance and be healed from it. *The cross dramatically reveals the problem of ignorant killing, to inoculate us against doing the same thing.*

Salvation history seems to lead people into the very darkness that they seek to overcome. There, they learn its real character, and how to unlock it from the inside. (p. 208)

- What is your response to Fr. Richard's framing of "the crucifix as a *homeopathic* image"? What new facets of understanding and/or empathy does that reveal for you?
- How would it be for you to walk into the darkness with Jesus at your side? What would change for you? What might be easier, or harder, about being in that experience?
- Write a prayer that describes a resistance you would like to develop through gazing on the crucifix.

14. Reflection

Today this is perhaps what we would call "grief work," holding the mystery of pain, looking right at it and learning deeply from it, which normally leads to an uncanny and newfound compassion and understanding. The hospice movement and the exponential growth in bereavement ministries throughout many of the churches are showing this to be true—but look how long it has taken us to rediscover such wisdom. (p. 209)

- What is your experience with "grief work"? What has it taught you about "holding the mystery of pain"? If grief work is new to you, what feelings arise in you as you consider the need for it?
- What is your experience with (and/or what have you heard about) hospice and/or bereavement ministry? How have these experiences and conversations impacted your understanding of and feelings about pain and death?
- Describe the wisdom to be found in "the mystery of pain."

15. *Lectio* Practice

I believe we are invited to gaze upon the image of the crucified *to soften our hearts toward God, and to know that God's heart has always been softened toward us, even and most especially in our suffering. This softens us toward ourselves and all others who suffer. (p. 209)*

Slowly read aloud the quotation above four times, following these instructions.

1. With the first reading of the text, allow yourself to *settle in* to the exercise and familiarize yourself with the words. Read the text out loud, very slowly and clearly. Pause for a breath or two before moving on.

2. For the second reading, *listen* from a centered heart space and notice any word or phrase that stands out to you.

3. After a few moments of silence, read the text a third time, *reflecting* on how this word or phrase is connected to your current life experience. Take a minute to linger over this word or phrase and allow it to engage your body, heart, and awareness of the world around you.

   You may want to speak a response aloud or write something in your journal.

4. For the final reading, *respond* with a prayer or expression of what you have experienced, inviting the infinite wisdom of God to support you in places of unknowing, confusion, desire, or hope.

16. Reflection

We usually dealt with human anxiety and evil by sacrificial systems, and that has largely continued to this day. Something has to be sacrificed. Blood has to be shed. Somebody has to be killed. Someone has to be blamed, accused, attacked, tortured, or imprisoned—or there has to be capital punishment—because we just don't know how to deal with evil without sacrificial systems. Such systems always create religions of exclusion and violence because we think it is our job to destroy the evil element. (p. 210)

- When have you witnessed someone declaring that "blood has to be shed"? What was the situation? What was the "evil" that needed to be expunged? What were your feelings about it at the time, and how do you feel about those circumstances now?

- In what ways has your church or religious community bought into the need for "exclusion and violence...to destroy the evil element"? How do you feel, thinking about this? If there were no consequences to your speaking up, what would you say or do about this? What might you be willing to say or do anyway?

17. Reflection

Historically, we moved from human sacrifice to animal sacrifice, to various modes of seeming self-sacrifice. Unfortunately, it was not usually the ego self that we sacrificed, but most often the body self as its vicarious substitute. (pp. 210–211)

- When were you taught about self-sacrifice in your family of origin? What were you taught about self-sacrifice in your church or religious community? What were your feelings about these teachings at the time, and how have they changed over the years?

- Describe your relationship with your body. In what ways do you sacrifice it? In what ways do you abuse it? In what ways do you honor it? What societal and spiritual teachings lie behind these attitudes?

- What would you like to change in your relationship with your body?

18. Reflection

As long as we can deal with evil by some other means than forgiveness, we will never experience the real meaning of evil and sin. We will keep projecting it over there, fearing it over there, and attacking it over there, instead of "gazing" on it within ourselves and weeping over it within all of us.

The longer we gaze, the more we will see our own complicity *in* and profitability *from* the sin of others, even if it is the satisfaction of feeling we are on higher moral ground. Forgiveness is probably the only human action that demands three new "seeings" at the same time: I must see God in the other, I must access God in myself, and I must see God in a new way that is larger than "an Enforcer." (p. 211)

- In what ways do you think about evil as "over there"? What are you learning about the consequences of this viewpoint?
- In what ways are you recognizing your "complicity *in* and profitability *from*" evil? What are you learning about the wisdom and opportunities in taking this viewpoint?
- Which of Fr. Richard's "three new 'seeings'" seem most difficult for you and why?

19. Reflection

Christianity is the only religion in the world that worships the scapegoat as God. In worshiping the scapegoat God, we should gradually learn to stop scapegoating, because we also could be utterly wrong, just as "church" and state, high priest and king, Jerusalem and Rome—the highest levels of authority—were utterly wrong in the death of Jesus. (p. 211)

- When have you been "utterly wrong" about something? What happened, and what were the results? In what ways was scapegoating involved? What did you learn about yourself at the time? What do you see now, looking back on it after reading *Things Hidden*?

- What would need to happen in your heart, your church, and your society for each to "gradually learn to stop scapegoating"? In what way could you make a start in at least one area?

20. Reflection

We all have to face the embarrassing truth that *we ourselves* are our primary problem. Our greatest temptation is to try to change other people instead of ourselves. Jesus allowed *himself* to be transformed and *thus* transformed others. (p. 212)

- Recall a recent occasion when you tried to change someone else. What were the circumstances and the reasons behind your efforts? What happened, and what were the results? Looking back, consider what you might have done to change yourself instead of trying to change the other person. What difference might that have made? What lessons do you see in this reflection?

- In what ways can you be more open to allowing yourself to be transformed? What lessons can you take from making Jesus your role model?

21. Reflection

Most Christians—Catholic, Orthodox, and Protestant—do not realize that what is commonly accepted as the mainline opinion—of Jesus's death as an atonement or heroic "sacrifice" of some type—was not the only Christian opinion in earlier centuries. This "majority opinion" was developed by early church fathers, and later championed by Saint Anselm, Saint Thomas Aquinas, and the mainline Catholic tradition. (p. 213)

- What are your thoughts and feelings about the "mainline opinion—of Jesus's death as an atonement or heroic 'sacrifice'"? How has it shaped your understanding of the crucifixion and your feelings about the relationship between Jesus and God, and between God and humanity? How have these feelings and understandings shifted over time?

- What is your response to reading that this "was not the only Christian opinion in earlier centuries"? What thoughts and feelings arise in you now—regardless of whether you've read or heard about this fact before?

22. Reflection

John Duns Scotus was not swayed or limited by the numerous metaphors of ransom, debt, redemption as "buying," blood sacrifice, payment of price (the Hebrew *goel*), or "purchased in blood" vocabularies that we frequently find in the Bible, in both the New Testament and the Hebrew Scriptures....

I would assume that Duns Scotus saw such language for the metaphors that they were: images that would have spoken powerfully to a people formed by temple sacrifice, animal offerings, and a quid-pro-quo kind of mind. (p. 214)

- What are your responses to the metaphors Fr. Richard lists here? Which of them speak powerfully to you and why? Which of them turn your stomach and why?

- It is highly unlikely that you were "formed by temple sacrifice [and] animal offerings." What religious images have formed you? How have they influenced your understanding of the crucifixion? What modern-day social images and teachings have influenced your understanding of the crucifixion?

23. Reflection

Duns Scotus saw these metaphors as limited because they made God's redemptive action a *reaction* based on human sin *instead of God's perfect and utterly free initiative of love.* This he could not tolerate. Duns Scotus knew that God is in charge of history, not us, and surely not our sinfulness. (p. 214)

- What is your response to this paragraph? What is new to you or a revelation here? What confirms something you know well, or might have sensed but couldn't articulate?
- What does this explanation tell you about the human desire to be in control and "in charge of history"? Describe how this desire has shaped your own life and attitudes.
- What difference does it make for you and for the world that God is initiating love instead of reacting to human sin?

24. Reflection

I would like to think Duns Scotus got his concept of free will from the concepts of biblical election and chosenness, concepts discussed above. Choice is absolutely free and arbitrary on God's part, and not in any way rational or determined. (p. 215)

- Have you previously considered the fact that God also has "free will"? What arises for you as you read this here?

- What is your response to the idea that God is not limited by our "rational or determined" understanding of events? In what ways is this freeing for you? In what ways is this challenging or frightening for you?
- What would it mean for you if God is indeed "arbitrary"? How would that change your relationship with God? What difference does it make in your response to realize that arbitrary response is about love, not condemnation?

25. *Lectio* Practice

In summary, *whatever happens to Jesus is what must and will happen to the soul:* incarnation, an embodied life of ordinariness and hiddenness, initiation, trial, faith, death, surrender, resurrection, and return to God. Such is the Christ pattern in which we all share, either joyfully and trustfully (heaven), or unwillingly and resentfully (hell). (p. 216)

Slowly read aloud the quotation above four times, following these instructions.

1. With the first reading of the text, allow yourself to *settle in* to the exercise and familiarize yourself with the words. Read the text out loud, very slowly and clearly. Pause for a breath or two before moving on.

2. For the second reading, *listen* from a centered heart space and notice any word or phrase that stands out to you.

3. After a few moments of silence, read the text a third time, *reflecting* on how this word or phrase is connected to your current life experience. Take a minute to linger over this word or phrase and allow it to engage your body, heart, and awareness of the world around you.

You may want to speak a response aloud or write something in your journal.

4. For the final reading, *respond* with a prayer or expression of what you have experienced, inviting the infinite wisdom of God to support you in places of unknowing, confusion, desire, or hope.

26. Reflection

Christ's *primacy* and *pattern* are ironically undone and even made unnecessary when all that really matters is the last week of his life. We could get that impression from such movies as Mel Gibson's *The Passion of the Christ.*

Instead, "Through *his goodness, revealed* to us in Christ Jesus, he *showed us* how infinitely rich God is in grace, saving us by pure gift... so that we are God's work of art, created in Christ Jesus to live the good life as, from the beginning, he had meant us to live it" (Ephesians 2:7–10). *Jesus is not the afterthought here, but the forethought, the first thought, the distilled icon of all that God is doing in creation.* (p. 216)

- What impact does this reading have on your understanding of why Jesus came to live among us? What does it mean that the crucifixion was not the focal point or the reason for the incarnation?
- If "we are God's work of art," what needs to change in the way you view yourself? If God "had meant us" to "live the good life...from the beginning," what needs to change in the way you live your life? In what ways could you more fully believe in, welcome, and embrace goodness?

27. Reflection

Jesus, of course, communicates this Godself most graphically and dramatically on the cross itself. There *we see and learn to trust* the free offer of God's love in a brutal, yet utterly compelling, image. It assaults the defended psyche, mind, and heart. Self-giving "love calls forth love in return," my Father Francis would say.

The trouble is that we emphasized paying a cosmic debt more than communicating a credible love, which is the utterly central issue. The cross became more an image of a divine *transaction* than an image of human *transformation*. (p. 217)

- To what extent is the cross a paradoxical tool for communicating grace and love? What can you understand in this image and what remains a mystery? What do you wrestle with here and what do you welcome?

- How does the cross "assault" your "defended psyche, mind, and heart"? What defenses does it overcome, and how? What grace is thereby allowed in?

- In what ways have you viewed the cross as evidence of "a divine *transaction*"? In what ways have you viewed the cross as "an image of human *transformation*"? What is shifting now in your understanding and your feelings as a result of reading this portion of *Things Hidden*?

28. Contemplative Sit

Leading in with the quotation below, practice a contemplative sit. You may wish to set a timer or digital prayer bell for twenty or twenty-five minutes, so that you know when to finish.

- Seat yourself in a quiet area.

- Ground yourself and allow your breathing to settle.

- Notice any tightness in your shoulders and neck and allow any tension in your muscles to relax.

- Allow your back to rest in an aligned, neutral position.

- Once you are settled, read the following passage aloud—this is the opening text for your sit:

The Son of God is presented as *reacting,* whereas a free and loving God would always *act* from God's own primordial and eternal truth. *Divine love is not determined by the worthiness of the object but by the goodness of the subject.* (p. 217)

- Continue your sit in silence—focusing on your breath, connecting with your body, or by practicing any other method with which you are familiar.
- Allow thoughts, feelings, and sensations to arise, exist, and then fall away while you keep your attention open and large, connecting to that much deeper consciousness.
- Remember, there is no goal. There is no right or wrong way—simply *be* present to what *is* in the moment.

Once finished, you may wish to journal your reflections on this experience.

29. Reflection

In Franciscan parlance, once again, *Jesus did not come to change the mind of God about humanity; Jesus came to change the mind of humanity about God.* This grounds Christianity in love and freedom from the very beginning. It creates a very coherent and utterly attractive religion, which draws people toward lives of inner depth, prayer, reconciliation, healing, and even universal "at-one-ment," instead of mere sacrificial atonement. Nothing "changed" on Calvary, but *everything* was revealed so we could change! (p. 218)

- In what ways has reading *Things Hidden* made Christianity more attractive to you?

- In what ways has reading *Things Hidden* made Christianity more challenging for you?
- Which of the faith life elements Fr. Richard lists ("inner depth, prayer, reconciliation, healing, and even universal 'at-one-ment'") are most enticing to you and why?
- Which of the faith life elements Fr. Richard lists ("inner depth, prayer, reconciliation, healing, and even universal 'at-one-ment'") are most demanding for you and why?

30. Reflection

Consequently, we have an energetic basis for a joy-filled and mystical Christianity, as Franciscanism always preferred. According to a nonviolent atonement theory, God is not someone we need to fear or mistrust.... Our only desire is "to fall into the hands of [such a] living and loving God" (Hebrews 10:31). But, like any trust fall, first we need to trust the one who is going to catch us. (p. 218)

- To what extent do you trust God? How and why has that shifted over the years? What impact has reading *Things Hidden* had on your trust level?
- What was your sense of the Franciscan tradition (beyond garden statuary of St. Francis and the birds) before reading *Things Hidden*? In what ways has Fr. Richard changed or enlarged your understanding of Franciscanism? How has that impacted you?
- Is "a joy-filled and mystical Christianity" appealing to you? Why or why not? What would need to shift in you for you to embrace this description of the faith life more fully?

31. Reflection

Is dominative power *our humanly preferred* way of dealing with our problems? (We *must* ask that question!) A violent theory of redemption legitimated punitive and violent problem solving all the way down—from papacy to parenting. There eventually emerged a huge disconnect between the founding story and the message of Jesus itself. (p. 219)

- Respond to Fr. Richard's question at the beginning of the paragraph. What does your response reveal about yourself and your perspective on your fellow humans?

- If you can do this safely, recall where in your life you have witnessed and/or experienced "punitive and violent problem solving" legitimated by Christianity. What feelings arise for you as you recall such events or exchanges? What messages did you receive and how do they still impact you?

- How has this "theory of redemption" impacted your faith life and your understanding of the nature of God?

32. Reflection

If God solves problems by domination, coercion, and violent demand, then we can too. Grace, mercy, and eternal generosity are no longer the very shape of God, as the Trinitarian nature of God seemed to say. Free will, grace, and love became less admirable than some theoretical cosmic justice, law, and blind obedience. We end up making God very small and drawing the Godhead into our own ego-driven need for retribution, judicial resolution, and punishment. Yet that's exactly what Jesus came to undo! (pp. 219–220)

- When and why have you wanted to solve problems "by domination, coercion, and violent demand"? To what extent was God a role model for this? What did you learn about yourself by acting in this way?

- What is your perspective on obedience, to humans and to God? How do you respond to the idea that Jesus was obeying God when he was crucified? How does/has this idea influenced your experience of the Christian faith?
- Explain in your own words how Jesus "came to undo" what Fr. Richard describes here.

33. Reflection

The many who learned how to pray, look, and listen...just gazed upon the crucifix long enough—and they *knew*. They knew it was all OK. They knew "Jesus died for our sins," but not through any needed heavenly transaction or convincing Bible quotes. *They knew it by gazing upon the one that we have pierced*, praying from a place of needed mercy, and allowing the Love which changed them from the bottom up. (p. 221)

- How do you explain the sentence, "Jesus died for our sins"? What individuals and/or church communities influenced your understanding? How is your understanding similar to and/or different from Fr. Richard's explanation?
- Have you met people who "knew it was all OK"? What was their impact on you and why? What have you learned from such people?
- To what extent are you able to allow God to change you? What experiences and/or understandings have helped you reach this point? In what ways are you still closed to or resisting God's love? Do you want that to change, or not?

34. *Lectio* Practice

The cross is about refusing the simplistic win-lose scenario and holding out for a possible win-win scenario. The cross is refusing to hate or need to defeat the other because that would be to continue the

same pattern, reciprocate the violence, and stay inside of the inexo-
rable wheel that the world has always called normal. (p. 221)

Slowly read aloud the quotation above four times, following these instructions.

1. With the first reading of the text, allow yourself to *settle in* to the exercise and familiarize yourself with the words. Read the text out loud, very slowly and clearly. Pause for a breath or two before moving on.

2. For the second reading, *listen* from a centered heart space and notice any word or phrase that stands out to you.

3. After a few moments of silence, read the text a third time, *reflecting* on how this word or phrase is connected to your current life experience. Take a minute to linger over this word or phrase and allow it to engage your body, heart, and awareness of the world around you.

You may want to speak a response aloud or write something in your journal.

4. For the final reading, *respond* with a prayer or expression of what you have experienced, inviting the infinite wisdom of God to support you in places of unknowing, confusion, desire, or hope.

35. Reflection

The cross moves us from the rather universal myth of redemptive violence to a new scenario of redemptive suffering.

On the cross of life, we accept our own complicity and cooperation with evil, instead of imagining that we are standing on some pedestal of moral superiority. (p. 222)

- To what extent is "the scenario of redemptive suffering" new or familiar to you? How would you explain it to others? How would you articulate both "our own complicity and cooperation with evil" and the hope that Fr. Richard shares?

- When have you stood on a "pedestal of moral superiority"? What was the issue? How did you feel, standing on that pedestal? Are you still there, or have you climbed down? Who or what experience helped you learn to climb down?

36. Activity

The mystery of the cross teaches us how to *stand against* hate without *becoming* hate, how to oppose evil without becoming evil ourselves. Can you feel yourself stretching in both directions—toward God's goodness and, also, toward recognition of your complicity in evil? If you look at yourself at that moment, you will feel crucified. You *hang in between*, without resolution, your very life a paradox, held in *hope* by God (see Romans 8:23–25). (p. 222)

- Stand in front of a mirror. Reach one arm out to the side in one direction, "toward God's goodness." Call to mind a recent experience of grace and imagine it there, just out of reach beyond your fingertips. Breathe deeply.

- Keeping the first arm up, reach out your other arm to the side in the opposite direction, "toward recognition of your complicity in evil." Recall a recent moment when you recognized you were complicit in evil in some way. Breathe deeply.

- With both arms still outstretched, look in the mirror and see your cruciform stance. Breathe deeply.

- Notice your body's reactions to standing in this way. How do your shoulders and arms feel? What other body parts are you feeling and why? What is your inner response to holding this position?

- How is it for you to *"hang in between"* your own goodness and evil?

- When you can no longer maintain this position, bring your arms to your sides and stand for a minute longer, facing the mirror, looking into your eyes. What thoughts and feelings arise?

- You may wish to reflect in your journal following this exercise, focusing both on your experience of the activity and "your very life a paradox, held in *hope* by God."

37. Reflection

The mystery of the cross reveals that *the opponent is not evil, but rather a symbol of a greater evil of which he or she is also a victim!* Please think about that. The mystery of the cross takes a great capacity for empathy and forgiveness, and probably is a sign of fusion with God. On the cross, we agree to carry that victim status together with Jesus. We agree to bear the burden of human evil, of which we *all* are victims, and in which all are complicit. (p. 222)

- To what extent can you accept the idea that "evil" people are also victims of an evil system? What is your response to this idea? What impact does it have on your view of others?

- In your own words, explain how Christians "agree to carry that victim status together with Jesus." In what ways would you choose to "bear the burden of human evil"? In what ways would you resist it?

- What capacity do you have "for empathy and forgiveness"? What experiences have honed that capacity for you? What feelings arise in you when you read this "probably is a sign of fusion with God"?

38. Contemplative Sit

Leading in with the quotation below, practice a contemplative sit. You may wish to set a timer or digital prayer bell for twenty or twenty-five minutes, so that you know when to finish.

- Seat yourself in a quiet area.
- Ground yourself and allow your breathing to settle.
- Notice any tightness in your shoulders and neck and allow any tension in your muscles to relax.
- Allow your back to rest in an aligned, neutral position.
- Once you are settled, read the following passage aloud— this is the opening text for your sit:

The mystery of the cross is saying that human existence is neither perfectly consistent...nor is it total chaos.... *Human existence, though, is filled with contradictions.* To hold the contradictions with God, with Jesus, is to be a Christian and to share and participate in the redemption of the world (Colossians 1:24). It feels like a *forgiving* of reality for being what it is. (p. 223)

- Continue your sit in silence—focusing on your breath, connecting with your body, or by practicing any other method with which you are familiar.
- Allow thoughts, feelings, and sensations to arise, exist, and then fall away while you keep your attention open and large, connecting to that much deeper consciousness.

- Remember, there is no goal. There is no right or wrong way—simply *be* present to what *is* in the moment.

Once finished, you may wish to journal your reflections on this experience.

CHAPTER TEN

Mutual Indwelling

1. Contemplative Sit

Leading in with the quotation below, practice a contemplative sit. You may wish to set a timer or digital prayer bell for twenty or twenty-five minutes, so that you know when to finish.

- Seat yourself in a quiet area.
- Ground yourself and allow your breathing to settle.
- Notice any tightness in your shoulders and neck and allow any tension in your muscles to relax.
- Allow your back to rest in an aligned, neutral position.
- Once you are settled, read the following passage aloud— this is the opening text for your sit:

"It is not what a person says, but the level from which they say it, that determines the truth of a spiritual statement." A spiritually mature person could use the word *perfection* and know they are talking about God's perfection abiding in us. An immature person will think of it as a moral achievement that they can attain by trying harder. (pp. 225–226)

- Continue your sit in silence—focusing on your breath, connecting with your body, or by practicing any other method with which you are familiar.
- Allow thoughts, feelings, and sensations to arise, exist, and then fall away while you keep your attention open and large, connecting to that much deeper consciousness.

- Remember, there is no goal. There is no right or wrong way—simply *be* present to what *is* in the moment.

Once finished, you may wish to journal your reflections on this experience.

2. Reflection

Our goal is not personal or private wholeness, which is clearly impossible anyway, yet it has been offered as an achievable goal for Western individualists for some centuries now. This is at the heart of our problem, and, in my opinion, has fostered massive withdrawal from Christianity.

Where the text finally points, leads, and calls is to the total mystery of divine union—and nothing less. (p. 226)

- To what extent has your goal been "personal or private wholeness"? What is your response to Fr. Richard's declaration that this is "clearly impossible"?
- In what ways do you agree with Fr. Richard that this goal "is at the heart of [Christianity's] problem"? What examples would you use to illustrate or refute this?
- Describe "the total mystery of divine union" in your own words, based on both your prior experience and what you have learned in reading *Things Hidden*. What do you notice?

3. Reflection

Only those who have begun to experience election, grace, forgiveness, love, union, and relationship will use the Bible fittingly. Without these, the Bible is and has been much more a problem for humanity than any kind of gift. It remains the mere wineskin, but not yet the wine. (p. 226)

- When have you witnessed people using the Bible in a problematic way? What happened and what was your response? How has reading *Things Hidden* influenced your thoughts on the use of the Bible?

- When have you used the Bible in a problematic way? What was the context and what were others' responses? How has reading *Things Hidden* influenced your perspective on your use of the Bible?

- When have you witnessed people using the Bible "fittingly"? What happened and what was your response?

- In what ways do you think you could use the Bible more "fittingly" as a result of reading *Things Hidden*?

4. Reflection

My assumption in this entire book is the same as that of John in his First Letter: "It is not because you do not know the truth that I am writing to you but because you know it already" (2:21). There is an Inner Knower called the Holy Spirit (John 14:17).

I am assuming and totally relying upon the Divine Indwelling to "teach you and remind you of all things" (John 14:26). (p. 227)

- Think back on your journey through *Things Hidden*. Recall at least one time when you had a sense of "I knew this already" as you read the text. What are your thoughts and feelings about learning in this way, and relying on your "inner Knower"?

- What is your response to Fr. Richard's declaration that he's "relying upon the Divine Indwelling" to "teach you and remind you"? How open are you to that Divine Indwelling and why?

- Start a prayer to, or start a conversation with, that Divine Indwelling. What arises within you in response?

5. Reflection

"Anyone who has will be given more, and they will have more than enough; but from anyone who does not have, even what they have will be taken away" (Matthew 13:12). *A deep consciousness multiplies insight and feeds on holy yearning; narrow consciousness actually destroys both.* It is so important to have the "beginner's mind," which, ironically, the child has more than the adult (Matthew 18:2–4). We have to "change," Jesus says, to get *back* there. (p. 228)

- What is your response to Jesus's words at the beginning of this paragraph? How has your response been impacted by your reading through *Things Hidden*?

- How open are you to change in general? How open are you to change in your spiritual life in particular? What would it mean for you to "have to 'change'"?

- How can you cultivate "beginner's mind" in the days and weeks ahead? In what ways do you desire and/or resist getting "*back* there" to the mind of a child?

6. Reflection

We could say that from then on, the whole Bible is trying to return us to the Garden. By the end (Revelation 21–22) it becomes the New Jerusalem, where there is no temple, but only the River of Life and the Trees of Life, where even "the leaves are for the cure of the pagans" (22:2) and where "God lives among humans" (21:3). (p. 228)

- What is it like to view the Bible from beginning to end in this summary fashion? In what ways is it appealing to view this very big picture, and in what ways is it challenging for you?

- Imagine for a few minutes what it would be like for God to live among humans. How would that work, and what impact would it have on your life? What thoughts and feelings arise for you as you consider this?

7. Contemplative Sit

Leading in with the quotation below, practice a contemplative sit. You may wish to set a timer or digital prayer bell for twenty or twenty-five minutes, so that you know when to finish.

- Seat yourself in a quiet area.
- Ground yourself and allow your breathing to settle.
- Notice any tightness in your shoulders and neck and allow any tension in your muscles to relax.
- Allow your back to rest in an aligned, neutral position.
- Once you are settled, read the following passage aloud— this is the opening text for your sit:

The Garden, you see, is the symbol of unitive consciousness. We cannot objectively be separate from God. We all walk in the garden whether we know it or not. We came from God and we will return to God. Everything in between is a school of conscious loving. (p. 229)

- Continue your sit in silence—focusing on your breath, connecting with your body, or by practicing any other method with which you are familiar.
- Allow thoughts, feelings, and sensations to arise, exist, and then fall away while you keep your attention open and large, connecting to that much deeper consciousness.
- Remember, there is no goal. There is no right or wrong way—simply *be* present to what *is* in the moment.

Once finished, you may wish to journal your reflections on this experience.

8. Reflection

Many of the journeys before that point are journeys away from the center, where we literally become "ec-centric." These are the recurring biblical texts of fall and recovery, hiddenness and discovery, loss and renewal, failure and forgiveness, exile and return.

Fortunately, we are always being led back to the real Center to find who we really are: to find ourselves in God. (p. 229)

- Return to the chart of your life journey that you created in Activity #9 of Chapter One. Prayerfully sit with it, noticing the times when you journeyed "away from the center." Recall, in each case, how you were "led back to the real Center." What do you notice? What thoughts, feelings, and/or prayers arise in you?

- Which of the recurring biblical text themes ("fall and recovery, hiddenness and discovery, loss and renewal, failure and forgiveness, exile and return") resonate most for you and why? Which themes do you find most repellent and/or challenging and why?

9. Reflection

That humble productivity and slow efficiency on God's part is called "the economy of grace" or the good news. Here, God fills in all the gaps, everything is used, and nothing is wasted, not even sin. It leads to a worldview of abundance and enoughness. Buying and selling is a cheap substitute, and always leads to a worldview of scarcity, judgmentalism, fear, and stinginess. Why would anyone want to live there? And yet many, if not most, of us do. (p. 230)

- What is your response to Fr. Richard's statement that not even sin is wasted? How do you think God has used your sins over the course of your life? How do you feel about this?
- Can you believe that not even society's sins are wasted? Why or why not?
- What holds you back from "a worldview of abundance and enoughness"? What steps would you like to take to change that?

10. Reflection

Yes, there is "a new heaven," but there is also "a new earth" (Revelation 21:1). What more fitting meaning could the "Second Coming of Christ" have except that humanity becomes "a beautiful bride all dressed for her husband" (Revelation 21:2)? Union is finally enjoyed and God's win-win story line has achieved its full purpose. What a hopeful end to history! (p. 230)

- What difference does it make that there is "a new earth" as well as "a new heaven"? How does that influence your perspective on "getting" to heaven?
- Regardless of your gender, ponder the idea of being "a beautiful bride all dressed for" Christ. What thoughts and feeling arise for you? In what ways does this align with your concept of divine union and in what ways does it clash?
- To what extent can you believe in Fr. Richard's "hopeful end to history"? What is your response to this scenario?

11. Reflection

The full biblical revelation has given us the history within the history, the coherence inside of the seeming incoherence. If we don't get this inner pattern, then religion becomes simply aimless anecdotes—just little stories here and there, with no pattern or direction. (p. 231)

- What impact has reading *Things Hidden* had upon your awareness and understanding of the "full biblical revelation"? Describe any new coherence you have glimpsed through this process.
- Which "little stories here and there" now have "pattern or direction" for you as a result of reading *Things Hidden*? Which little stories still feel disjointed? How might you explore and learn more about their role in the "inner pattern"?

12. *Lectio* Practice

The clear goal and direction is mutual indwelling, where "the mystery is Christ within you, your hope of glory."...In this mutual indwelling, we no longer live as just ourselves, but live in a larger force field called the Body of Christ....As Charles Williams...explained, the "master idea" of Christianity is *co-inherence*. But it takes a long time to allow, believe, trust, and enjoy such wonder. (p. 231)

Slowly read aloud the quotation above four times, following these instructions.

1. With the first reading of the text, allow yourself to *settle in* to the exercise and familiarize yourself with the words. Read the text out loud, very slowly and clearly. Pause for a breath or two before moving on.

2. For the second reading, *listen* from a centered heart space and notice any word or phrase that stands out to you.

3. After a few moments of silence, read the text a third time, *reflecting* on how this word or phrase is connected to your current life experience. Take a minute to linger over this word or phrase

and allow it to engage your body, heart, and awareness of the world around you.

You may want to speak a response aloud or write something in your journal.

4. For the final reading, *respond* with a prayer or expression of what you have experienced, inviting the infinite wisdom of God to support you in places of unknowing, confusion, desire, or hope.

13. Reflection

We are facing a crisis of meaning today that becomes very quickly a crisis of hope and a scrambling for external power, perks, and possessions. The world will be destroyed by two things, it seems to me: greed and violence. Perhaps this is obvious. That's why great spiritual teachers will always teach us, first, to live a simple life, to not take more than our share, so that communion and community, brotherhood and sisterhood, are possible. (p. 232)

- Where do you encounter "a crisis of meaning" and "a crisis of hope" today? What is your response to these crises? What might Christ be calling you to pray, speak, and/or do about this?
- In what ways are you still lured by "external power, perks, and possessions"? What changes would you like to make in your attitude toward these cultural icons?
- What is your "share"? In what ways could you live a simpler life? In what ways are you called to share with your community?

14. Reflection

Then a good spiritual teacher will teach us some kind of inner disciplines to reveal and heal inner fears and aggression, which are transformed, quite simply, into happiness. I call it contemplation or non-dual consciousness, which is achieved by abiding in God, who already abides in us. It is the Holy Spirit. (p. 232)

- What kinds of inner disciplines do you currently practice? What shifts or changes might you need to make for these to be more effective? Are you called to try something new?
- Define "happiness." What cultural baggage or traditional expectations surround this term for you? What about "happiness" do you need to release or embrace?

15. Reflection

The things Jesus talked about constantly, like living a simple and nonviolent life in this world, like forgiveness and inclusivity, are still considered fringe thinking by many Christians. How strange that we have the capacity to not see what is taught so clearly by the one we consider our teacher. (p. 232)

- What would you consider the most transformative thing you've learned from this book? How has it helped you to see Jesus's teachings and/or God's love more clearly?
- What message(s) from *Things Hidden* are you called to share more broadly with your faith community? Which of Jesus's teachings support the message(s)? In what ways can you share the message(s)?

16. Reflection

In a sense, the Christ is always too much for us. He's always "going ahead of [us] into Galilee" (Matthew 28:7). The Risen Christ is leading us into a future for which we're never, ever, ready. Only little by little do we become capable of mutuality, of communion, of pure presence. (pp. 232–233)

- In what ways is this paragraph reassuring? In what ways is this paragraph frustrating? What assumptions about your capacity to know, feel, and act are being challenged here? What do you imagine Jesus would have to say to you about this?

- In what way(s), "little by little" have you become more "capable of mutuality, of communion, of pure presence" as a result of reflecting deeply on the lessons in *Things Hidden*?

17. Reflection

We don't have to figure it all out or get it all right ahead of time. We just have to stay on the journey. All we can do is stay connected. We don't know how to be perfect, but we can stay in union. "If you remain in me and I remain you," Jesus says, "you can ask for whatever you want and you're going to get it" (see John 15:7). When we are connected, there are no coincidences anymore. (p. 233)

- In what ways is this paragraph reassuring? In what ways is this paragraph frustrating? What can you do to "stay connected"? What can you do to "stay in union"?

- How has reading *Things Hidden* influenced your concept of being connected with Christ and remaining in Christ? What still confuses or challenges you? How might you take that to prayer?

18. Reflection

The Eucharist is actually a homeopathic medicine, whereby we eat and drink our own death ahead of time, in loving union with his death, instead of always demanding that others die. We preemptively walk right into the mystery of death and, like him, trust its other side, which is resurrection. (p. 235)

- What is your response to Fr. Richard's declaration that "Eucharist is actually a homeopathic medicine"? What thoughts and feelings come up for you? How does this give you a new perspective on "communion"?

- What does it mean that "we eat and drink our own death ahead of time"? In what ways is this freeing? In what ways is this binding?

- In your own words, reflect on how walking "right into the mystery of death" leads to resurrection.

19. Reflection

In contemplation, there is no argument about Real Presence. People who can simply be present will know about presence, union, and even ecstasy, and they would not think of denying God's availability in the material world. They know that Eucharist is a distilled and focused statement about the objective Incarnation. It is the ongoing Incarnation continued in space and time that tells creation what it is afraid to believe: "My dear people, we are already the children of God, but what we are to be in the future has not yet been revealed. All we know is that when it is revealed, we shall be like him" (1 John 3:2). (p. 237)

- What do "presence" and "union" mean to you now, after reading this book? How do you understand God's presence and "availability in the material world"? What feelings does this raise in you?

- How has your understanding and experience of the Eucharist changed as a result of reading *Things Hidden*?

What "has not yet been revealed" to you? What is it like to sit with the mystery?

20. Reflection

We all are saved in spite of ourselves—and for one another. It never was a worthiness contest. If God is love and if grace is true, then what exactly is the cutoff point? When is God's arm too short to save (Isaiah 50:2)? Are there any who have achieved worthiness and do not need saving? Name them, please. (p. 237)

- Respond to Fr. Richard's questions. Have your responses changed as a result of reading this book?
- "If God is love and if grace is true," how does your life need to change to match these truths?
- If we are all saved "for one another," how does your attitude toward and response to others need to change?

21. Reflection

In human history, it seems to me so very little is really resolved or solved, settled or answered. We live in the in-between, holding the tensions, discovering and even loving the paradoxes, realizing we ourselves *are* the contradictions visualized by the geometric image of the cross.

That living space, the ultimate liminal space, is called faith, and Jesus praises it even more than love. (p. 238)

- What is it like to come to the end of a book and have so many "big picture" questions remain unresolved? What does that say about God? What does your response say about you?
- What perspective(s) in you might need to shift and align more fully with the cross?

- What does it mean that "Jesus praises [faith] even more than love"?

22. Activity

Slowly, prayerfully read aloud Symeon's hymn (pp. 239–240). Pause when a word or phrase catches your attention, but do not do anything further. Move on when you are ready. Line by line, be present to the hymn without needing to do anything more.

23. Contemplative Sit

Leading in with the quotation below, practice a contemplative sit. You may wish to set a timer or digital prayer bell for twenty or twenty-five minutes, so that you know when to finish.

- Seat yourself in a quiet area.
- Ground yourself and allow your breathing to settle.
- Notice any tightness in your shoulders and neck and allow any tension in your muscles to relax.
- Allow your back to rest in an aligned, neutral position.
- Once you are settled, read the following passage aloud— this is the opening text for your sit:

God's power is precisely used for mercy throughout the evolving Bible. What could possibly be allowed to frustrate this divine desire or God's capacity for true victory? Paul states, "Nothing!" (p. 238)

- Continue your sit in silence—focusing on your breath, connecting with your body, or by practicing any other method with which you are familiar.
- Allow thoughts, feelings, and sensations to arise, exist, and then fall away while you keep your attention open and large, connecting to that much deeper consciousness.

- Remember, there is no goal. There is no right or wrong way—simply *be* present to what *is* in the moment.

Once finished, you may wish to journal your reflections on this experience and your overall experience of working through this Companion Guide to *Things Hidden*. Conclude your journal entry with some form of thanks for all that has occurred during this time.

Every encounter with *Things Hidden* will be unique because every person brings a different mix of experiences, understandings, and awareness to their engagement with Scripture. Therefore, using this Companion Guide in a group setting can further deepen and enrich your experience. To assist in this process, we offer the following guidelines.

Facilitator

The role of facilitator is essential to the health and effectiveness of a practice group. The facilitator may not be able to fully participate in the group reflections and practices, as they are responsible for setting a hospitable, organized, and calming tone, together with keeping the group on track.

Such leadership comes with its own growth opportunities and reasons to celebrate, so facilitators are encouraged to engage with a person or community who will support and pray for them throughout their time as a facilitator.

Practical Considerations

The size of a practice group should be between eight and twelve members, not including the facilitator.

The facilitator will need to have on hand at each meeting:

- bell or gong
- candle
- Bible

- *Things Hidden* book
- Companion Guide

To prepare for each week's session, the facilitator will need to read ahead, choose an appropriate number of practice elements in the Companion Guide, and determine the amount of time to be allotted to each element. Each week, the facilitator will wish to inform the group about which practices will be used the following week, so that group members can read that portion of *Things Hidden*.

Each week, the facilitator will need to:
- organize the group logistics, including room setup;
- do the related reading in *Things Hidden*;
- introduce and explain each practice during the group session;
- track time for each practice;
- monitor the group sharing;
- be the contact point for questions or concerns throughout the course of the sessions.

Pair Sharing and Group Discussion

We recommend developing a balance of group work, pair sharing, and solo reflection for each group session. Obviously, different types of practices will lend themselves to different types of participation.

Group Work involves group sharing in a circle using a "talking stick," reflective *Lectio* practice, and contemplative sit. These are times to broaden participants' experience and understanding through sharing.

A "talking stick" is introduced by the facilitator at the first session. It can consist of something as simple as an actual stick, a stone, or a paperweight. During group sharing, individuals pass around the talking stick and take turns sharing; only the one holding the talking stick speaks.

Pair Sharing gives individuals an opportunity to share what is true for them with one other person and to practice being an attentive listening presence to their partners. Many reflection exercises in this Companion Guide can be followed by pair sharing.

Solo Reflection is time for individuals to process the content as it relates to their own lives and journal what arises for them.

Time

Allow ninety minutes for the first session and include an opportunity for each participant to share something about themselves and why they have chosen to join the group at this time. Subsequent sessions should be structured to take no more than sixty minutes per session. It is important to begin and end on time, respecting both the facilitator's time and that of the group members.

The Spiritual Discipline of an Experiential/Embodied Group

The purpose of using this Companion Guide in a group is to facilitate a sequence of practices in which a group can engage together. The goal is for group members to contemplate more deeply on the content of the book, rather than using the book itself for group discussion.

Using the Companion Guide with a Group

The role of the facilitator is to keep the group on task, transition the group from one activity to another, and discourage the group from engaging in dialogical discussion and debate. The facilitator introduces the spiritual practices, facilitates contemplative sit and *Lectio*, and guides the group in the use of the talking stick as part of group sharing.

The first session is particularly important, as it will set the tone for how the rest of the group sessions will be facilitated. At the start of the first group session, the facilitator:

- welcomes the group;
- shares a little about themselves and why they are personally motivated to facilitate this group;
- communicates the start and end times of each session, and any comments on the location of each session (such as restroom locations);
- reminds group members to bring their copy of *Things Hidden*, the Companion Guide, a journal, a pen, and a Bible each week;
- describes the group focus (i.e., moving away from *discussion and debate* and toward *spiritual practices*);
- explains the types of exercises to be used in the group: Group Sharing (including contemplative sit, *Lectio*, and the use of a talking stick), Pair Sharing (including changing partners each week), and Solo Reflection;
- outlines the agreements for group participation:
  - Reading the book.
  - Respecting the group guidelines and the role of the facilitator.
  - No commenting or interrupting when a group member is sharing.
  - Holding confidentiality throughout and after the course of the group sessions, inside and outside the sessions.
  - Sharing *only* one's own personal story.

Three Types of Reflection

The facilitator may wish to share these descriptions of the following three types of reflection practices so that all group members hold the same expectations:

1. Solo Reflection

During solo reflection, individuals reflect on their own. The group members may move from their seats, as long as they remain within the meeting room/space. The solo reflection exercise is timed (e.g., from one to five minutes, as the facilitator determines). When appropriate, the facilitator can give the group a one-minute notice, so members have an opportunity to conclude their reflection.

2. Pair Sharing

In pair sharing, individuals meet with a partner. Individuals are asked to change partners each week, to avoid sharing with the same partner throughout the course of the weekly group sessions. The facilitator explains some benefits of sharing with a different partner each week (taking the risk of getting to know and be vulnerable with other people, being exposed to different perspectives and experiences). The facilitator will give pairs notice when half the sharing time is up, so that each person has time to both share and listen.

3. Group Work

Group work will include group sharing with the use of a talking stick, *Lectio*, and contemplative sits. These are forms of communal spiritual practices—a sacred way of interacting in community that emphasizes active listening to oneself and to others, rather than engaging in cognitive discourse.

Group Sharing Guidelines

As facilitator, you will need to notice and guide the energy and the pacing of the group as a whole. We recommend using these Group Sharing Guidelines and reading them to the group during the first session, and at other times as needed.

Group Sharing Guidelines
- Gather in a circle.
- Use the talking stick.
- Speak in the moment (try not to prepare something in advance).
- Speak from the heart (speak what is *true* for you, regardless of whether it is "right").
- Be lean of speech (share a few sentences at most, with time to pause and ponder in between).
- Listen from the heart (respect the honest sharing of others and listen in a way that moves you beyond thinking of what this means to *you*; instead, what does this mean to the person who is sharing?).
- Respect confidentiality in this sacred space (what is shared in the group *must* stay in the group; otherwise, the group cannot grow together).
- In group sharing, be mindful of not speaking or commenting when individuals are sharing. Practicing patience, by not speaking too much and listening in silence, is an important part of group sessions.

Lectio

As facilitator, you may want to read the text in advance of a session, so as to be familiar with the content. You may also wish to spend some time engaging in a *Lectio* of your own, using the text, as part of your preparation for the group session. This will give you a general sense of the timing and cadences of the *Lectio* that you will lead.

Review the *Lectio* instructions and calculate the time it will take for the *Lectio* practice, predicated on the number of group participants. (If there are ten members in the group, and there are 15 minutes allotted for the *Lectio* practice, 1–1.5 minutes of reflection per person is appropriate.)

Silent pauses are particularly important between reflections throughout the *Lectio* practices. (The speed at which you read and speak will guide, and affect, the experience of the group.)

Some group members may have never engaged in *Lectio* like this before, so it is important to ease their concerns at the start. If necessary, answer a question or two, then simply invite them to *experience* the practice, regardless of any concerns they may have.

Note: If you think it would be helpful, you may want to talk about your own experience of Lectio *practice. If you do share, be concise and speak from the heart.*

If the group struggles through the *Lectio* practice, remind them that *Lectio* is an invitation to move deeper through reflection, meditation, and prayer, so as to avoid discussion or analysis.

Contemplative Sit

Contemplative sit may be new to some members of the group. Familiarize yourself with the process ahead of time. Remind the group of the information on sit included in this Companion Guide. Determine the contemplative sit time in advance. Prepare the room ahead of time with a lighted candle and a prayer bell to gently indicate the start and end of the contemplative sit.

Note: You may wish to use a digital prayer bell from your cell phone or tablet meditation app.

Remind the group of the option to use a sacred word, such as Yah-weh or Je-sus, or simply invite them to focus on their breath—in and out—whenever distracting thoughts enter their minds, so as to bring them back to the present moment.

Some group members, who may have never engaged in contemplative sit, could struggle with the practice initially, so simply invite them to allow themselves to *experience* the practice, using the following script and pausing slightly after each sentence:

- As we begin our sit, let's take a few moments to notice our posture. Becoming comfortable in our seat, let's sit slightly forward, so that our spine is no longer touching the back of the seat. Let's become aware of both of our feet touching the floor, grounding us in the present moment. Let's focus on our back and our neck, allowing them to find their most aligned and neutral positions. Now, I invite us to lower our gaze and focus on a point on the floor in front of us. Or, if we feel comfortable, we may want to close our eyes.

- As we begin our contemplation, let's remember that we are not trying to "achieve" anything. There are no goals. We are simply becoming aware of this moment. Becoming aware of our presence in this moment. Noticing any distractions, thoughts, judgments, decisions, or ideas that cross our mind, we choose to let them go for now. We choose instead to focus on our moment-by-moment experience of being present to What Is. God's Presence. Deeper consciousness.

- As we become distracted, frustrated, or confused, we consciously return to offering up our moment-by-moment presence to God's Presence by using a sacred word or simply focusing on our breath. We know that God's Presence is already within us, whether we're aware of it or not.

Note: If you think it would be helpful, you may want to share your own experience of contemplative sit. If you do share, be concise and speak from the heart.

The instructions for contemplative sit are outlined every time it occurs in the Companion Guide. Here is a fuller set of instructions to guide those who are unfamiliar with the practice or wish some reminders on important points.

Opening Instructions

Leading in with the quotation below, practice a contemplative sit. You may wish to set a timer or digital prayer bell for five, ten, or twenty minutes, so that you know when to finish.

Seat yourself in a quiet area.

We presume that you will choose to sit in a chair or on a cushion on the floor/ground, but we are aware that this is not the best position for some people's bodies. Please adjust these instructions to meet your best contemplative position and posture.

Preparing the Body

There are many ways of preparing the body to engage in a contemplative sit. We have chosen a simple approach that is neither particularly strict nor technical. It will allow you to become aware of your body and, hopefully, to stay awake as you engage in the sit.

Ground yourself and allow your breathing to settle.

Notice any tightness in your shoulders and neck and allow any tension in your muscles to relax.

Allow your back to rest in an aligned, neutral position.

The phrase "ground yourself" has many possible interpretations and connotations. Here, it is an invitation to become aware of your presence on this earth, in this moment. You may want to find a position for your feet that helps you feel connected or literally "grounded." Some people remove their shoes and socks, while others engage in an outdoor sit so they can feel the sand, grass, or soil beneath their feet or tailbone. The invitation here is to become physically still and to notice the whole-body sensations you are experiencing.

We often carry stress and tension in our shoulders and neck. By taking a moment to become conscious of this, you will be better able to let go of some tension as you relax into your sit. If there are other areas in your body where you habitually hold tension, add a noticing of these parts to your practice.

The next instruction, regarding the alignment of your back, is simply to help with your posture so you do not injure yourself during the sit. Allowing your spine to rest in an aligned, neutral position can sometimes feel strange, which illustrates how often we unconsciously let it curve it into an unnatural position. You do not have to sit bolt upright, but be conscious of maintaining a good posture and remain alert to any bodily sensations you may experience.

It can be helpful to soften the focus of your eyes, allowing them settle on a point on the floor or ground a couple of feet away from you. Alternatively, you may wish to close your eyes. This serves to quieten one of your five senses and help you focus your attention during the sit.

Place your hands on the top of your legs or knees, palms up or down, in the way that is most natural or meaningful for you.

Reading

Once you are settled, read the passage aloud—this is the opening text for your sit (this quote is from the first Contemplative Sit in the Introduction):

> You will note that I use many Scripture citations with only a small comment, hoping that such a small comment will tease and invite you into deeper involvement with the text and context for yourself. I would love to inspire you to love Scripture, and go there for yourself, to find both your own inner experience named, and some outer validation of the same. (p. xv)

Each sit invites you to seat yourself in a quiet area, to settle down, and then to read a short excerpt from *Things Hidden*. This excerpt is designed to focus your attention and allow an open-hearted engagement with God. Even if you read all the instructions in silence, reading this excerpt aloud can be helpful for grounding you in the moment.

There is no particular goal or emphasis as you read the excerpt; you do not have to focus on the theology of the concept, and you do not have to grasp the excerpt in its entirety. Feel free to read it at face value, or to read it in the style of a *Lectio* text, focusing on a word or phrase that stands out to you.

When you feel ready, move on to the next step.

Focusing

There are many approaches to focusing during a contemplative sit. Here are some suggestions of methods that you may find helpful.

At times you will find it difficult to focus as you begin your contemplative sit. If this is the case, be patient with your thoughts, treating yourself with kindness and compassion. Then consciously choose to move the focus of your attention from your headspace down your body, first to your chest and then to your stomach and navel, the center of your body. Imagine your thoughts and your egoic mind descending to the "grounded" center of your body.

Bring your attention to your breath, moving in and out, without changing your breathing in any way. Choose to focus your attention on this bodily sensation instead of the swirling, repetitive thoughts or attention-grabbing emotions you may be feeling.

Remember Fr. Richard's words from chapter two:

> All great traditions teach some form of contemplation because it is actually a different form of knowledge that emerges inside the "cloud of unknowing." It is a refusal to eat of the tree of the knowledge of good and evil, and finding freedom, grace, and comfort in the not needing to know, which ironically opens us up to a much deeper consciousness that I would call the mind of God. That's because our small mind and lesser self is finally out of the way. (p. 38)

As you read through each script in successive contemplative sits, you may be drawn to certain phrases more than others, placing emphasis there as you read. This is perfectly fine. Your manner of speaking will help set the tone of your contemplative sit.

Refocusing During the Sit

Don't be surprised if you lose focus at times as you seek to open yourself to experiencing God's moment-by-moment presence. It is normal to be distracted during a sit, to feel bombarded by thoughts, to feel anxious or frustrated, or to want the sit to be over. This is all part of training your egoic mind to quieten. What is most important is how you respond once you become aware of this loss of focus and attention. Repeating the following lines (or others that you may wish to write for yourself) can preempt this happening:

"As I become distracted, frustrated, or confused, I consciously return to offering my moment-by-moment presence to God's Presence....No offering up is needed—I am offering in...into the silence...into each moment that I sit in contemplation."

One approach is to try not to let your attention attach to any thoughts, feelings, or sensations that may arise. Allow them to arise, exist, and then fall away while you keep your attention open and large, connecting to that "much deeper consciousness" (p. 38).

In addition, some people find the use of a sacred word to be helpful. Sacred words like Je-sus and Yah-Weh have been used for centuries. As Fr. Richard notes:

> Some Jewish scholars say that the consonants used in the spelling of YHWH are the very few that do not allow us to close our mouths around them, or even significantly use our lips or tongue; in fact, *they are very likely a brilliant attempt to replicate human breathing: YH on the captured in breath, and WH on the offered out breath!* (Stop reading and literally take a breath on that one!) (p. 140)

The sacred word you choose is up to you, as long as it is personally meaningful and will help you to refocus your awareness any time you become distracted. Some teachers encourage the use of short sacred words that are no more than three syllables in length (e.g., love, stillness, gratitude) while others are more concerned with the personal significance of the word, rather than its length.

Several approaches to the method of using a sacred word involve the constant repetition of a sacred word, akin to a chant or a mantra. Other approaches (such as Centering Prayer) use a sacred word as a focal point to return your attention to a position of openness and rest.[1]

If you prefer, you can simply focus on your breath—in and out—whenever distracting thoughts cross your mind. The approach of returning to your breath is the method given as part of the instructions for each sit.

Finishing Your Sit

The final instruction, after the closing bell has sounded, is to take some moments to process anything that may have come up for you during the sit. Journaling your experiences—from bodily sensations to thoughts and emotions—can be helpful to review as you grow in the practice.

---

1. Thomas Keating, "The Difference Between Centering Prayer and Dom John Main's Christian Meditation," *Contemplative Outreach*, November 2017, https://www.contemplativeoutreach.org/article/difference-between-centering-prayer-and-dom-john-mains-christian-meditation.

About the Author

Richard Rohr is a globally recognized ecumenical teacher whose work is grounded in Christian mysticism, practices of contemplation and self-emptying, and compassion for the marginalized. He is a Franciscan priest of the New Mexico province and founder of the Center for Action and Contemplation in Albuquerque, where he also serves as academic dean of the Living School for Action and Contemplation. Fr. Richard is the author of many books, including the bestsellers *Just This, What Do We Do with Evil?, The Universal Christ: How a Forgotten Reality Can Change Everything We See, Hope for, and Believe,* and *The Wisdom Pattern: Order, Disorder, Reorder.* The Center publishes Richard's Daily Meditations, free reflections emailed to hundreds of thousands around the world.